GARDEN TIME

SHOWING YOU HOW TO CREATE A BEAUTIFUL GARDEN

Mark Cullen

ISBN: 1-8960-9204-7

INFACT Publishing Ltd.
66 Portland St.
2nd Floor
Toronto, ON
M5V 2M8

Cover and text design and video digitization: Brant Cowie/ArtPlus
Cover Photography: Paterson Photographic Works Inc.

Photo credits: Cover courtesy of Plant Products Co. Ltd.;
p. iv Janet Davis; p. vi Gardenimport inc.; p. 8 Plant Products Co. Ltd.;
p. 16 Plant Products Co. Ltd.; p. 26 Plant Products Co. Ltd.;
p. 34 Gardenimport inc.; p. 43 Plant Products Co. Ltd.; p. 50 Janet Davis;
p. 58 Plant Products Co. Ltd.; p. 66 Janet Davis; p. 74 Janet Davis;
p. 86 Plant Products Co. Ltd.

Special thanks to Wendy Thomas; Dennis Flanagan of Weall & Cullen;
Darlene Sanderson, Jenny Hale and Dave Watson of Plant Products Co. Ltd.;
Dugald Cameron of Gardenimport inc., John Hill and Kevin Weir of
Nu-Gro Corporation; Patti Mills-Roy and Bob Vaillancourt of
Canadian Tire Corporation, Limited and everyone at CTV.
– M. C.

Printed in Canada by Metropole Litho

Contents

Introduction

Gardeners, even experienced ones, always seem to have lots of questions. Quite a few of them start with "when" and many more start with "how." For many gardeners, the last weekend in May is the time to plant out annuals, but when is the best time to plant perennials? to fertilize the lawn? to prune the roses? and how do you prune roses, anyway!

I'm glad that gardeners have such questions because it gives me a chance to write and talk about my favourite subject — gardening. One of the places I talk about gardening is on CTV's "Canada AM," where Dan Matheson joins me to discuss gardening techniques, favourite plants, and other gardening matters that interest us. But because it's television, we can do more than talk — we can show you just how to dig a hole, how to prune a rose bush, what various plants look like. We've put together this video of some of the most popular programs we've done so far, and I've written this book to accompany it.

In the pages of this book, you'll find additional information about the topics we cover in each segment so you'll be able to refer easily to it every year. I'll expand on the topic and tell you how to care for your plants throughout the growing season, what pests and diseases are likely to be a problem and how to deal with them, and how to prepare for winter. Included throughout the book are places for you to make notes as a reminder of the conditions in your own garden.

Gardens are as various and individual as the people who plant them, but, experienced or novice, it doesn't hurt to have a few basic principles under our belt and to remind ourselves of them now and then.

Not just good gardening practices but good design principles are at work here: the yellows add liveliness to the rosy and mauve colours. The tall and short plants provide the variety needed in such an intensive planting.

1 *Roses*

Many people believe a garden isn't complete without roses. And it's not surprising that so many gardeners feel this way — roses are one of the oldest cultivated flowers and have been a staple of European gardens since the Middle Ages. Over the centuries, their popularity has never lessened.

Breeders have provided us with increasing varieties suitable for just about every condition in colours in every increment from pure white through pink and yellow to the deepest richest red. You can get them scented or with only the hint of the famous rose scent. You can get plants that are compact, ones that ramble as a ground cover, climb up a host tree or trellis or stay neatly in a miniature growth.

Here in Canada, we're restricted to a certain extent by our growing conditions, but I think this makes growing roses even more fulfilling. Just think of the great variety of conditions we face across the country — cold winters and cool summers in the eastern provinces, fluctuating snow cover and winter temperatures with hot humid summers in the middle of the country, then the unpredictable seasons on the west coast. Yet gardeners in all these areas grow roses — lovely roses!

In the spring, pull the protective earth away from the stems. Just spread the earth around the bush.

Using sharp pruners and wearing gloves, cut back to green wood. Make all such cuts at a 45° angle.

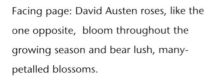

Facing page: David Austen roses, like the one opposite, bloom throughout the growing season and bear lush, many-petalled blossoms.

Assess your site, take into consideration your climate (see page 4 for information about zones), then have some fun doing research about the types of roses that have been bred for gardens such as yours. Giving roses the conditions they crave will pay off. Even if you grow just one rose bush in your garden, you'll find there's nothing to compare with the joy of watching the buds open into those amazing blooms.

Planting Roses

Planting roses takes some advance planning. Choose a site that will give the roses full sun, although it's possible to find some varieties that don't mind partial shade. If you have the space, give the roses their own bed — they don't like competing with other plants for nourishment. If this isn't possible, at least keep them away from trees and shrubs. The site should offer protection from strong winds, as well.

Prepare the planting area before you receive the plants, ideally a month or two before you want to plant in the spring or in the previous fall. Dig the bed well, as deeply as possible — don't be afraid to go to 60 cm (24 inches). Remove all weeds as you work the soil. Add as much well-rotted manure or compost as you can get your hands on.

The soil needs to be rich and should hold water but drain well. I know this sounds contradictory! Sandy soil drains well but doesn't hold water; clay soil holds the water too well and therefore doesn't drain. So you're aiming for a soil that will allow the water to move through it, drawing in oxygen to the roots, but will also hold the water to be released to the roots over a few days. See page 78 for more information on soils.

Most people plant their roses in the spring, but in milder parts of the country (Zone 6 and milder), you can plant them in the fall. Before you plant your new rose bush, put it in a bucket of water for up to 12 hours, letting it take in the moisture. If you find you can't plant the bush in its permanent location right away, temporarily plant it in a trench in the garden in its pot so that the roots are protected from the elements.

Have some well-rotted manure or compost on hand to backfill the hole after planting. Make the hole for planting wide enough to accommodate the root ball and deep enough so that all roots will be underground without being jammed. If the plant has been grown in a container, tease the roots out of the ball, especially if they have taken on the shape of the container. If you don't do this, you are condemning your rose to certain death — the roots will continue to grow in the shape they have taken on and will eventually strangle themselves. The budding union — the point where the rootstock and stem meet — is the most sensitive part of the plant, and requires winter protection. Follow planting depth and wintering methods for your zone.

Don't be afraid to be ruthless. This pruning will give your plant a wake-up call and encourage it to get growing.

Scratch in a handful or two of 8-10-12 fertilizer.

Spread the fertilizer so that it's directly above the spread of roots and it will go right where it's needed.

With your heel, make a well around the plant. This depression will hold the water and direct it to the roots.

Here are some guidelines for how close to plant roses. Miniature roses can be planted 20 cm (8 inches) apart; hybrid teas and floribundas, 90 cm (3 feet) apart; and shrub roses, 1.5 m (4 feet) apart. The newly planted bed might look pretty barren, but in the middle of summer even such seemingly generous open spaces can begin to look crowded. Also, you want easy access to your plants in the fall when you're preparing them for the winter, another good reason for not crowding them.

Put the plant in the hole, backfilling with the rotted manure or compost, working it into the surrounding soil. A handful of bonemeal is a good addition, too, for it will help the plant develop strong and healthy roots. Keep firming the soil around the roots, using your foot to stamp out air pockets. Finish with

Zones

I've indicated zones in planting charts to guide you in deciding whether a particular plant will grow in your area. The Canadian system of zones is based on the mean minimum winter temperature, mean maximum summer temperature, length of frost-free period, rainfall from June to November, depth of snow cover, and the strength of wind gusts. Let me stress again that these are guides. Conditions in your garden can vary by a zone or two, depending on how sheltered or exposed your garden is and a variety of other influences.

Zones are subdivided into parts a and b, b being slightly milder.

Zone 0b: La Ronge, Sask.; Thompson,Man.
Zone 1a: Gagnon, Que.
Zone 1b: Chibougamau, Que.; Timmins, Ont.; The Pas,Man.; Prince Albert, Sask.
Zone 2a: Noranda, Que.; Grande Prairie, Alta.
Zone 2b: Baie Comeau, Que.; Fort Frances, Ont.; Brandon,Man.; Regina, Sask.; Saskatoon, Sask.; Prince George, B.C.
Zone 3a: Thunder Bay, Ont.; Portage la Prairie,Man.; Winnipeg,Man.; Swift Current, Sask.; Calgary, Alta.; Edmonton, Alta.
Zone 3b: Edmunston, N.B.
Zone 4a: Sudbury, Ont.
Zone 4b: Corner Brook,Nfld.; Campbellton, N.B.; Quebec City, Que.; Trois Rivières, Que.; Sault Ste. Marie, Ont.
Zone 5a: Moncton, N.B.; Fredericton, N.B.; Ottawa, Ont.; Barrie, Ont.
Zone 5b: St. John's, Nfld.; Saint John, N.B.; Montreal, Que.; Kingston, Ont.
Zone 6a: Sydney, N.S.; Charlottetown, P.E.I.; Halifax, N.S.; Toronto, Ont.; London, Ont.; Kamloops, B.C.
Zone 6b: Yarmouth, N.S.
Zone 7a: Windsor, Ont.
Zone 8b: Vancouver, B.C.; Victoria, B.C.

This rose has barely survived a harsh winter. Don't give up too soon, though. Some first aid might save this one.

Trim, trim, trim! Cut off all the dead wood and clear away any remaining mulch.

It might not look very promising right now, but there's a chance you've just saved a plant. It's always worth the effort.

a top dressing of the manure or compost, and make a trench around the plant. This small depression will catch the water and help direct it to the feeder roots. Water thoroughly, let the water drain away, then water again. Add a mulch if you want, and water again. Continue thorough weekly watering for several weeks after planting, especially if rainfall is low.

Care in Spring and Summer

During the growing season, roses need frequent, deep watering. By frequent I mean once or twice a week, especially when it's been dry. By deep, I mean at least 2.5 cm (1 inch) of water at each watering. Use a rain gauge or any container set out to catch some of the water to help you see how much water this is. When the container has about 2.5 cm (1 inch) in it, your roses will be well watered.

Pruning roses is a thorny issue, in more ways than one! Most roses can be pruned in the spring because they form flowers on the new growth, but a few flower on the previous season's growth. If you have one of the latter, prune it as soon as flowering finishes. If you've been having trouble getting your rose to bloom, maybe you've been pruning it at the wrong time of year.

Always prune just above an outward-facing bud; this encourages the new growth to grow away from the centre of the plant, allowing better air movement — and thus healthier plants.

We all dream of rose bushes smothered in fragrant blooms but roses are greedy so we have to be sure they're well fed. Feed your roses monthly with an 8-10-12 fertilizer; give the last feeding in July.

Cut off fading blooms — a practice known as deadheading — to encourage the rose to continue blooming for as long as possible.

Pests and Diseases

A common disease that attacks roses is black spot. You'll notice it on the leaves and, true to its name, it causes small black spots to appear, usually on lower leaves first. The leaves turn yellow before falling off. The spore that causes the disease survives the winter, often on fallen foliage, so good fall cleanup is one way to avoid the problem. Rust is another spore disease; it shows up on the under leaf as an orange-brown powder. If you are hit with one of these diseases, pick off the affected leaves but do not put them in the compost; put them in your garbage for regular pickup. A mulch also helps to keep the spores from reaching the leaves. Otherwise, try a commercial fungicide or insecticidal soap.

Aphids can be a problem on roses. Control them with an insecticidal soap or simply rub them off the affected parts. Be sure to wear garden gloves when you do this!

Winter Preparation

The first step in winter protection actually comes when you buy the plant: make sure that it will survive in your climate. Many varieties are being bred for harsh climates — in fact, some of the hardiest plants have been bred by Agriculture Canada. Look for the Explorer series of roses; the plants bear names such as John Cabot amd William Baffin. If you're a beginning gardener, buy plants that are hardy in your zone. There'll be time to push the limits and experiment as you gain experience in this wonderful hobby, but for now, you want to feel successful.

Once you've had the first harsh frost, prepare your roses for winter by removing the foliage and pruning them by about half. Spray with dormant spray then mound some soil around and over the plant. If you don't want to use soil from another part of the garden, use peat moss. You can also use purchased rose collars to help keep the soil in place. If you use rose collars, you can fill them with straw or leaves instead of soil. Soil will freeze so you may want to save your rose collars for your best plants. In the spring, remove the material you've used for winterizing and follow the steps I showed Dan.

Cut back long branches of climbers so they don't whip around in winter winds. Some gardeners even take climbers down from the trellis and, after cutting them back slightly, lay them on the ground for the winter.

Don't forget that one of the best insulators is snow. Let the snow drift around your protected roses to help moderate the temperature of the soil beneath. More harm is done to plants that are subjected to fluctuating temperatures in the winter than is done by cold.

What Kind of Rose to Plant

Floribunda, grandiflora, hybrid tea . . . it almost sounds like a kid's skipping rhyme. Don't be overwhelmed or put off by these designations. Here is a brief introduction to some of the names you'll come across when you start looking for the perfect rose for your garden.

Climber and Rambler: Quite hardy; many are repeat blooming or everblooming; climbers grow up; ramblers grow sideways or down and can be used as groundcover.

Floribunda: Bushy; flowers grow in clusters; continuous flowering; less demanding to grow than hybrid teas; can be used for a low hedge.

Grandiflora: Taller than hyrbid teas; flowers similar to hybrid tea but larger; need winter protection.

Hybrid Tea: Bushy; single or double flowers; one flower per stem; usually fragrant; great variety of colours; grow to 1 m (3 feet) or higher in milder climates; flower intermittently; need good winter protection in most parts of the country.

Miniature: 25 to 37 cm (10 to 15 inches) tall; small double or semi-double flowers; good for growing in containers.

Shrub: Less showy flowers than other roses; some are fragrant; can be put in border with other plants; can grow to 1.2–1.5m (4 to 5 feet high); some bloom on old wood; very hardy.

Tree or Standard: Hybrid tea or floribunda rose grafted on to a single long (1 m / 3 foot) upright stem; nice in a formal garden; need good winter protection in most parts of the country.

Notes

2 *Planting an Evergreen*

As we plan our gardens, we sometimes forget about evergreens; it's easy to get overwhelmed by the rainbows of colour and the blossoms of annual and perennial plants. But as we become more sophisticated in our gardening, the usefulness of evergreens quickly becomes apparent.

In the summer, they offer a cooling green to temper hot yellows, reds, and oranges or provide backdrops to show off cooler pale pinks, soft blues, and creamy whites. In the winter, they come in to their glory. They give visual delight when their branches are powdered in snow, as well as serving as windbreaks and providing protection for birds.

Texture, shape, and colour are elements to consider when designing your garden. Again the evergreens come to our rescue. Their needles can be short and spiky or long and feathery. The trees themselves come in a wide variety of shapes — small mounds or domes, pyramids or cones, stately columns, and weeping forms.

A towering spruce can draw the eye to the far reaches of a large garden and tie together the beds and plantings. In smaller gardens, dwarf varieties add accents and act as "bridges" between changes in colour schemes. Creeping evergreens can spill over rock gardens or out of containers.

One of my favourite gardening tasks – screening compost. You're left with a wonderful soil enhancer.

The large pieces remaining can go back in the compost bin or be mixed with other materials to make a mulch.

Facing page: Even in a small area, you can see the versatility evergreens offer.

I especially like the incredible range of evergreen colours you can find — blackish greens, blue greens, bronzy greens, gold greens, silvery greens, grey greens, and every shade in between!

Whether your garden is a large space or a small plot, there's an evergreen for you.

Planting Evergreens

Evergreens are best planted in the spring, although it is also safe to plant in the autumn, when they are going into a period of dormancy. You want to get them planted before the times when they suffer the most stress — in the heat of summer and the cold of winter. They can be planted in the spring as soon as you can work the ground up until the weather starts to get hot. Choose a spot where the soil is well-drained. Like many plants, evergreens prefer a soil that drains well but holds moisture.

In order to get your evergreen off to a good start, you're going to have to water it well after it's planted. The soil should hold moisture well. The best way to ensure that it will do so is to add organic matter such as well-rotted compost to the planting hole before you plant. The feeder roots will soon grow into this amended soil to absorb the moisture it holds.

Make the hole twice the width of the root mass. Fill this hole with the compost and dig it in well, then make a new hole for the evergreen. Tease the roots gently a bit — scarify them, in other words — to encourage them to grow out into their new surroundings. Insert the plant so that the top of the root ball will be level with the ground. You will have to use some judgement regarding the depth of the hole, for the soil under the root ball will settle a bit when you water. Backfill with the soil you removed to make the hole, and with the ball of your foot firmly pack it down to get rid of air pockets and to be sure the plant is well stabilized in the earth. Make a final check to be sure the top of the root ball is still level with the surface of the ground.

As I mentioned earlier, watering is extremely important, so give the newly planted tree a good soaking and add some transplanting fertilizer to get the roots going. Follow the directions on the package when using the transplanter. As a final precaution, add a good layer of mulch to help conserve the moisture. Mulching materials include bark chips, partially decomposed compost, leaf mould, well-rotted manure, even newspapers (although newspapers will have to be held down with a layer of pebbles or soil).

A final word about choosing evergreens: be sure you know how large the tree is going to grow. How many of us have seen — perhaps even lived in — houses that were overpowered by a monster evergreen? I can guarantee that when that little tree was planted in the middle of the front lawn, no one was

Carefully slide the plant from the pot. Roots growing through the bottom can be removed if they hamper its release.

Dig a planting hole that is just slightly deeper and wider than the root ball.

Fill the hole with a soil enhancer such as triple mix – usually a combination of compost, manure, and loam.

Scratch the roots to loosen them up. They will be encouraged to grow into the new soil more easily.

thinking about its size in ten or twenty years. On the other hand, if you buy a dwarf variety, stop dreaming about majestic pines! Be clear about the part you want your evergreen to play in your garden, plan accordingly, and buy wisely.

Care in Spring and Summer

During the growing season, water your evergreens well. The feeder roots are likely to be in the top 15–30cm (6–12 inches), and they need to be well soaked. If your soil is on the sandy side, you will need to water more frequently than if you have a clay soil. In either case, long waterings are better than frequent shallow ones.

Hedges versus Fences

You might want to hide an unattractive view, have more privacy in your garden, or need to divide sections of your garden. Two solutions spring to mind: fences and hedges.

Good fences might make good neighbours but they also give a no-nonsense message: Keep out! That's not to say they have to be unfriendly. A climbing rose spilling over a fence will gladden the hearts of passersby. Clematis and fences are made for each other. Even chain link fences are improved when morning glories are scrambling over them. Make your boundaries clear without offending anyone by using your fence as a way of extending your growing space with vines and climbers.

Fences take some upkeep and have to conform to local bylaws. And don't forget those neighbours — involve them in decisions regarding mutual fences.

Hedges offer a somewhat softer message. A hedge of roses is a beautiful sight first and a deterrent to taking a short cut across the lawn second. They can be informal, as in the rose hedge, or more formal, as in a smartly pruned row of cedar.

Hedges will need watering, fertilizing, and possibly several prunings a year. They'll likely take a few years to reach maturity, but once grown, an evergreen hedge will look attractive all year.

A perfect fit! The hole is just big enough to accommodate the root ball. Back fill with the rest of the soil.

Firm the soil around the plant. It's important to get out any air pockets so the roots are in contact with the soil.

All that's needed now is a good watering. Don't hold back. Continue watering through the summer, especially in dry periods.

Even though the roots of mature evergreens can travel deep into the soil, they don't always get all the nutrients they need. Fertilizing will give you healthy plants with rich colour and quick growth. Apply the fertilizer — a balanced one such as 10–10–10– is best — anytime from early to late spring.

Evergreens need only light pruning. Most of them grow into attractive shapes naturally, but every now and then you might want to give Mother Nature a hand. If you prune just before a period of rapid growth, the pruning cuts will be hidden quickly and you'll have denser growth on a more compact plant.

Pests and Diseases

Although an evergreen doesn't drop its needles the way a deciduous tree drops its leaves, it's quite natural for some of an evergreen's needles to die and drop every year. So get to know your tree; recognize when it's going through a natural stage so you can distinguish those times when it's suffering. Evergreens generally have few insect or disease problems, nevertheless, you might find yourself with an ailing tree or shrub. What are symptoms you should be concerned about and what can you do to restore health?

Needles are sticky or deformed: The problem is likely aphids or mites. Aphids can be washed off the plant with a stream of water; you can also apply an insecticide. You can check for mites by holding a piece of white paper under a branch and shaking it. If you see small yellow, green, or red dots moving about on the paper, you've got mites. Use a miticide right away, because mites can cause great damage.

Needles have a crusty, sticky, or waxy growth: Scales, small sucking insects, cover themselves with a waxy shell and produce the sticky liquids that accumulate on the needles. You might have noticed reduced growth, yellow leaves, and some dieback of stems before you actually see the scales. Prune and destroy infected branches. Use a dormant oil early in the spring; in early summer spray with an insecticide.

Needles and twigs have an orange jelly: A disease called rust is attacking your tree. Cut off and destroy any infected growth. Spray with a fungicide.

Winter Preparation

Give your evergreens a good deep watering in the late fall. They easily dry out in the harsh winds of winter, so this will help them through. It's especially important to protect first-year evergreens in the winter, but older trees will also benefit from being sheltered. Either loosely wrap burlap around the plant or build a frame of burlap or canvas to set around the tree. Many people object to seeing these shrouded objects in the winter, but if you've spent good money on a plant you love, you'll want to protect your investment. As an extra safety precaution, spray your evergreens with an antidesiccant to help prevent moisture loss. An antidesiccant on its own, however, will not be sufficient.

Another type of winter protection involves binding the branches of small upright evergreens. This is very important for small trees that are planted close to a house; they could suffer from melting ice dripping on them and refreezing or from sheets of snow sliding off the roof and breaking their limbs. Use a strong garden twine or netting to bind them.

Mulching will help new plants survive the often killing effects of periods of freezing and thawing. The mulch not only conserves moisture, but moderates the soil temperature.

Notes

3 *Annuals and Hanging Baskets*

his is where most of us start our gardening experience. We buy a few pansies, some petunias, a marigold or two, and before we know it, we're hooked on gardening — all thanks to annuals. Whether growing in containers or filling empty spots in a bed, annuals have a place in every garden.

One of the most popular uses for annuals is in pots such as a strawberry planter or hanging baskets. This type of planting offers the gardener amazing versatility. You can change the plant combinations from season to season; you can move the pots around the garden to change colour schemes or to provide accents in different spots. Most vegetables are annuals, too, so don't be afraid to tuck a lettuce plant in among the geraniums! It will look attractive and provide the fixings for a summer salad. Cherry tomatoes will soon fill a hanging basket on their own. You can also make planters that contain nothing but herbs. These are nice to have just outside the kitchen door.

There are some special tricks to growing in containers, so I'm going to tell you how to have lush blooms all summer. And if, for some reason, a plant or two fails, it's easy to pop in a replacement or even to replant the whole container. Although I'll be talking about hanging baskets, part of the fun of container

The cheery face of a Bingo pansy, a frost-resistant plant that can be set out early.

Facing page: Geraniums are perfect for containers, which dry out quickly.

Impatiens are usually shade plants, but breeders have given us some for sunny spots. Sunshine impatiens, above, is one such new variety.

gardening is the wide variety of pots, bowls, troughs, and boxes you can grow in and then finding the perfect plant or combination of plants to put in them.

Planting a Hanging Basket

Container planting, which includes hanging baskets, is intensive planting — a lot of plants are competing for a limited supply of nutrients and water, but some easy-care techniques will keep your plants happy. Before we get to that, let's look at some plants to use in your hanging basket.

Pansies are tolerant of light frosts and are one of the earliest annuals that can go outdoors — I've seen them in barrels on the west coast as early as March. So don't feel too sorry for the ones you see peeking through a late spring snowfall — they'll be just fine. They come in a wide variety of colours, so you can mix and match them with one another and with other flowers.

Impatiens keep on blooming without being deadheaded, their colours are clear and sparkling, and they tolerate poor soil. They don't like to get too dry, though, and they are quite sensitive to frost. We generally think of them as shade plants, but the New Guinea varieties do well in the sun. This makes them good additions to a hanging basket because you can mix them in with other plants that need the sun.

Ivy geraniums are another traditional plant for hanging baskets. Like ivy, they have a trailing habit and look fabulous tumbling over the edges of baskets. These varieties come in slightly more muted colours than other geraniums. The Balcon ivy geraniums are more heat- and drought-tolerant than other ivy geraniums. And for foolproof container growing, don't forget the lovely fibrous begonias.

Set off your colourful flowers with some foliage plants. Here's where you can get really creative. Many of the following plants are frost sensitive, but during the summer they'll do just fine. At the end of the summer, take a few cuttings and grow them indoors. Ivies, spider plants, and asparagus fern all add cool green interest to the basket and provide textural interest; the asparagus fern is airy and arching, spider plants have an interesting striped leaf, and ivies come in a wide array of leaf shapes and colours. Dusty miller, which grows upright, adds a nice colour change and softens hot colours with its grey-green velvety foliage.

Now that you know which plants you're using, choose your basket. The easy one is the plastic holder into which you drop a pre-formed mat of cocoa fibre. If you want to start from scratch, use a wire basket. Have on hand some sphagnum moss that's soaked in water overnight or at least a couple of hours in warm water. Put a layer of the moss on the bottom of the basket and work it up the sides to the top; it won't look as neat on the outside as the cocoa mat, but

A hanging basket is one of the best ways of showing off annuals.

Using sphagnum moss, line the bottom and start up the sides. You can start inserting plants as you go if you want.

Pull the roots through the moss so they will be in contact with the soil. You might have to knock the existing soil off the roots.

An easy alternative is the preformed liner and plastic holder. Whichever you use, the planting medium must be a patio mix.

• •

once the plants get growing, it won't matter. A wire basket 40 cm (16 inches) across and 25 cm (10 inches) deep can take as many as 20 plants. A solid plastic hanging basket will take fewer as the sides won't be available for planting.

Use a prepared patio mix as the growing medium. These prepared soils are light in weight, contain a balanced mix of nutrients and fertilizers, and will provide good drainage. Do not use garden soil — it's heavy and will cause you nothing but grief. It contains weed seeds, insects, and possibly diseases. You can mix some polymer crystals, sold under various brand names, in to the patio mix. They absorb water, turn into a gel and swell to many times their dry state. Over time, they release the water to the plants, cutting down on the amount of watering you have to do. Another method of

Defining Terms I

If you're a beginner to gardening, you probably feel overwhelmed by some of the terminology, so let's look at some terms you'll come across when buying seeds or seedlings. I'll define some more gardening terms on page 62.

Annuals: Plants that complete their life cycle in one season. They germinate, flower, set seed, and die in that time. New plants might appear the next year, germinated from the seed set by the plant. Some common annuals: pansies, petunias, cosmos, impatiens.

Hardy annuals: Seed for hardy annuals can be sown directly into the ground in the fall or early spring as soon as the ground can be worked.

Half-hardy annuals: Half-hardy annuals will succumb to frost. Seed for half-hardy annuals should be started indoors and the seedlings should not be planted out until all danger of frost is past.

Perennials: Perennials live more than two years. They go dormant in the winter but put on new growth in the spring. Some common perennials: peonies, lilies, Oriental poppies, hostas, astilbes.

Biennials: Biennials complete their life cycle in two years and then die. Some biennials: foxglove, hollyhock, sweet william.

Balcon geraniums make an attractive addition to hanging basket plantings as they spill over the edges.

Fibrous begonia, on the left, is foolproof, whether in sun or shade. It makes a nice colour contrast with dusty miller, right.

You can have a different kind of ivy for each basket or container if you want. Add some tall plants to offset the trailing habit of the ivy.

saving water is to put a layer of plastic over the moss before you add the patio mix and plants. This will prevent the patio mix from drying out and will help to stop a freshly watered basket from dripping excessively. If you add the plastic liner, don't forget to slit it to accommodate any plants that are going in the sides of the basket.

Just before you start planting, take a look at the selection of plants before you. Give some thought to the shape the basket will take as the plants begin to grow. Trailing plants look best planted in the sides of the basket and around the top edge. Plants that grow upright can be put in the top centre. Have an idea of how the plants are going to be spaced in the basket before you get going.

Now it's time to start planting. Fill the basket about half full with the patio mix. Start inserting the plants for the sides between the ribs. Gently remove some of the soil from their roots so they are easier to insert. Push the roots gently through the moss and into the patio mix. Continue planting up the sides of the basket, adding more patio mix as you go. Always firm the soil around the roots. Give the basket a deep watering and add a layer of mulch if you want, to conserve moisture.

Now you can hang the basket and admire your handiwork!

Care in Spring and Summer

Because all sides of a hanging basket, especially a wire basket, are exposed to the elements, they tend to dry out quickly. If you've used some of my water-conserving tips in planting, you've already given your plants a good start. Nevertheless, many hanging baskets will need watering every day, especially if the weather has been hot and windy.

Some patio mixes contain slow-release fertilizers, but if your patio mix doesn't, fertilize the basket every ten to fourteen days with 20-20-20.

Picking off spent flowers — a practice called deadheading — will keep the flowering plants producing more blossoms. Sometimes plants such as lobelia begins to get leggy during the mid to late summer. Just shear it off a bit and it will reward you with renewed growth.

Pests and Diseases

Plants in hanging baskets, because they're planted intensively and are more affected by the elements, are under more stress than plants in beds or even in larger containers. And plants under stress are more likely to fall prey to pests and diseases. Keep a close eye on your plants as you water them. Check the undersides of leaves as you pick off spent blooms.

A good insecticidal soap will take care of many insect problems you're like-ly to encounter in hanging baskets — aphids, spider mites, whitefly are the most common. Occasionally you might be bothered by mildew in a hanging basket, although because hanging baskets usually have good air circulation, it's unlikely to be a serious problem. However, if you've had a humid summer with few dry winds, you might find a powdery residue on the leaves of plants, a sig-nal your plants have been affected by mildew, a fungus disease. Provide better air circulation, if possible, and water baskets in the morning, avoiding wetting the leaves. If this fails, use a commercial fungicide. Make sure you take care when using all pesticides and fungicides.

Winter Preparation

As the days grow shorter and nights grow cooler, your hanging basket might begin to look rather sad. Its days are nearly over. But don't just toss those plants on the compost — take some cuttings and grow them over the winter in preparation for next year's hanging basket.

Put the moss and patio mix in the compost, and wash the basket before storing it.

The Right Plant for the Right Spot

Success with annuals doesn't depend much on the zone in which you live. The extremes of temperatures don't affect them, since they don't spend the winter in the ground. The chart on the facing page will help you choose some annuals for your particular conditions. Some plants appear in more than one column because they need a combination of specific conditions.

Notes

. . . .

Sun	Part Sun	Shade	Moist	Dry
Ageratum	Coleus	Begonia	Begonia	Blanketflower
Alyssum	Browallia	Forget-me-not	Cupflower	California poppy
Baby's breath	English daisy	Impatiens	Heliotrope	Blanketflower
California poppy	Monkey flower	Monkey flower	Nasturtium	
Candytuft	Nicotiana	Pansy	Portulaca	
Cosmos	Pansy	Sunflower		
Cupflower				
Dusty miller				
Geranium				
Heliotrope				
Lobelia				
Morning glory				
Marigold				
Pinks				
Petunia				
Portulaca				
Sweet pea				
Sunflower				
Verbena				
Zinnia				

OUR GROWING CONCERN...

Hand tools

Watering

Garden Club™

Introducing 'Garden Club™' — a bright new label in yard fashions

Canadian Tire is pleased to debut an exclusive new line of premium gardening supplies. Look for our distinctive dark green and cream logo on the best in a wide range of gardening needs including hand tools, hoses, nozzles, sprinklers and accessories, flower bulbs, grass seed, fertilizers, chemicals, patio lights and more — the 'Garden Club' is a growing concern!

Bulbs and Rose bushes

Fertilizers, Chemicals and Grass Seed

LE95-463

Imagine how green your garden will grow with Plant-Prod fertilizers!

Imagine the bright, colourful flowers, the plump, healthy vegetables, the rich green lawn, the beautiful shrubs...

Plant-Prod water soluble fertilizers can make it all come true for you: And they're so easy to use!

Find out why most professional growers depend on Plant-Prod... and start growing your dream garden this year.

Plant Products Co. Ltd.
314 Orenda Road
Brampton, Ont.
L6T 1G1

plant prod ®

Made in Canada

4 *Perennials*

Perennials are those mainstays of the garden, the plants we can depend on to return year after year. Although their blooming time is usually shorter than annuals', every year I welcome with affection old-fashioned perennials such as peonies, irises, poppies, and daylilies.

Most perennials have an added mixed blessing. They increase over the years, taking up more and more space so that — here's where the mixed blessing is — we have to divide them. It can be hard work, especially if you've let them get too crowded, but you'll have lots of new plants to trade with friends or put elsewhere in the garden.

Because perennials stay in one spot for many years, you need to prepare the beds well the first time around. After that, some minimal upkeep is all that's necessary to keep your plants happy.

There are so many perennials to choose from it's often difficult to control yourself when thinking about what to plant. Narrow your choices down by reviewing your growing conditions and site, deciding on the colour scheme you want to implement, and perhaps considering a few principles of garden design (see page 70).

Dianthus, or pinks, make a lovely edging for a sunny informal garden. I especially like their clove scent.

Nestle a few saxifrages among rocks in a dry setting to show it off to perfection. It won't object to this treatment at all.

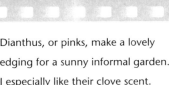

Facing page: It takes planning to have continuous bloom in the perennial bed, but look at the pay-off!

With careful planning, you can have a succession of blooms from your perennials so that as one stops blooming, another a bit farther down the bed is ready to burst into flower. By doing a bit of research, you can find perennials that will make your garden lively from May right through September.

Planting a Perennial Bed

I'm going to assume that you're starting a perennial bed where only grass existed before and that you're doing it in the spring. Choose a place that isn't close to a tree, for several reasons; first, the tree will cast shade, which will restrict the choice of perennials, and second, the roots will rob the soil of nutrients, so that the plants are always competing for moisture and nutrients. Mark off the shape of the bed with an old hose or old rope. Move it around until you're happy. There are no right or wrong shapes for beds, only personal preference. A straight edge along the front of the bed can be every bit as attractive as an undulating one.

Now start digging! Turn the sod over, then shake it off before adding it to your compost pile. Before you start enriching your soil, search out any weeds that remain, especially parts of roots. They'll just set off growing even more strongly than before. By sifting through this bed several times, pulling out weeds and rocks, you'll be getting to know your garden really well. Are you finding lots of earthworms? Congratulations! You've got a great gardening helper working for you. If you haven't got many worms, this is a sign your soil needs some help in the way of organic matter. Once the bed is quite clean, start digging in peat moss and well-rotted compost or manure. Whether your soil is clay or sand, compost will improve it. And even if your soil seems perfect, with lots of worms, you should still add compost — I don't think it's possible to have too much organic material in a bed. Dig down at least 30 cm (1 foot) as you work these amendments in. Finally, rake the bed over to break up any lumps of earth that have made their way to the top.

If possible, wait for a slightly overcast day to plant; don't plant on a rainy day or when the soil is wet. Slide the plant out of its pot and put it in a hole prepared just to the size of the root ball. Firm the soil around the plant well, so that the plant is stable and there are no air pockets. Water well. A layer of mulch — bark or wood chips, compost, cocoa shells, dried grass clippings, straw, pine needles, and so forth — will help to moderate the temperature of the soil and conserve moisture.

It's tempting to plant perennials too closely — they may not seem too close right now, but in a couple of years, they'll be fighting for space. Read carefully and follow the planting instructions that come with new plants or consult some garden reference books to see how much space they'll take up as mature plants and plant accordingly.

Good friable soil: the goal of every gardener. Friable? That means it's crumbly and easy to work.

Gently take the plant from its pot. If it's reluctant, turn it over and tap the bottom. Cup your hand to catch the plant.

Insert the plant firmly into a hole that's slightly larger than the root ball. Make sure the roots aren't twisted or jammed.

Firm the soil around the plant, bringing the roots into contact with the soil and filling any air pockets.

Care in Spring and Summer

The first year, your new perennials might not seem to be doing much. Next summer, though, you'll see good growth and bloom if you keep them well-watered this summer. Water deeply and infrequently rather than frequent shallow waterings. If it's hot and windy, you'll need to water more often than in still weather.

In the early summer, cut off dead heads and stems of perennials that have bloomed in the spring. In the case of bulbs, be sure not to cut the foliage — it's helping the bulb store energy for next year's blooms. Plants such as aubretia sometimes become straggly after blooming. Prune them back, using

Drying Flowers

Do you ever wish, in the middle of winter, that you could recreate the blossoms of summer? It's not that hard to do. The secret is to dry those summer blossoms for use in flower arrangements when our gardens are resting during the winter.

Some plants dry extremely well, so let's have a look at a few of these that can easily be grown from seed. Strawflowers like a sunny spot and are tolerant of hot dry weather. They produce a daisy-like, rather stiff flower. Pick the blooms on a dry day just as they are beginning to open; they will continue to open after picking. Statice has papery flowers of lavender, pink, blue, white, and yellow. It too grows well in hot dry weather. Pick when about two-thirds of the flowers have opened. Globe amaranth produces little flowers that look like clover heads. The colours are pink, white, purple and orange. Pick them when their buds have fully developed.

As a general rule, pick flowers for drying in the middle of the day. The plants should be dry so don't cut them after rain or a heavy dew. Strip leaves off the stems and tie them together in small loose bunches. Hang them upside down in a dark, well-ventilated room. It will take about 4–6 weeks before they are ready for arranging.

Divide perennials in early spring or fall. Cut them back, water well, and dig up a clump. Slice clump through the roots.

This bed of daylilies needs dividing. Around the edges, growth is vigorous but plants in the centre are depleted.

Daylilies are aggressive and need dividing every few years. This clump of roots will provide many offspring.

scissors or shears, to about a half of their original growth. You might even get another round of bloom out of them.

Plants such as delphiniums usually need staking. Be careful that you don't damage the plant's roots as you insert the stake.

Keep the bed well weeded. This is especially important because there is often more unplanted space in a new bed. Every time a weed pops up, it's stealing nourishment that could be going to your plants.

Pests and Diseases

The most irritating pest seems to be slugs. It seems everyone has a favourite way to get rid of this garden muncher — and some of them are pretty gruesome sounding! To repel slugs, take your choice of any of the following to sprinkle around affected plants: wood ashes, lime, diatomaceous earth, sand, or crushed eggshells. Or mount a foot patrol and hand pick them at night (not for the squeamish gardener). Some people put out a shallow saucer of beer; the slugs are attracted to it, frolic about in it, then die. Hostas are a favourite of slugs.

Earwigs are another pest that chews holes in leaves. They are reddish brown and have pincers emerging from their abdomen. They like to congregate in small dark spots so you can trap them in such things as old hoses or corrugated cardboard. In the morning, collect these traps and shake the contents into soapy water to kill the earwigs.

Aphids (very small insects with pear-shaped bodies) leave a sticky residue on plants. Mites, which are nearly invisible (look for them on the underside of leaves), leave a silky web on the foliage of plants. Often a strong stream of water will knock aphids and mites off the plant. Once on the ground, they die. A severe infestation of aphids or mites can be treated with insecticidal soap.

Winter Preparation

Your new perennials' first winter is an important one. Don't be too quick to prune the plants, although it's important to keep things tidy as you prepare for winter. But stalks and stems left standing will help hold snow, an excellent insulator. The best thing you can do for your perennials is to give them a good layer of mulch no matter where you live in Canada. Snow cover is uncertain in many parts of the country, and without the snow your plants will be more vulnerable to winter winds and the damage of freezing and thawing cycles.

Wait until the ground has begun to freeze, then put on a layer of any of the mulches I mentioned above. Cover the plants with at least 5 cm (2 inches) of the material. In subsequent winters, it isn't as important to mulch unless you live in a region where snowfall is iffy or there are frequent swings between above- and below-zero temperatures.

The Right Plant for the Right Spot

Here are some common perennials, categorized by zone and preferred growing condition.

Zone	Sun	Part Sun	Shade	Moist	Dry
2	Lady's mantle	Bleeding heart	Hosta	Monkshood	Yarrow
3	Oriental poppy	Lungwort	Spotted dead nettle	Primrose	Golden margeurite
4	Sundrop	Astilbe	Columbine	Jack-in-the-pulpit	Hens-and-chickens
5	Flax	Foxglove	Gentian	Clematis	Sea holly
6	Threadleaf coreopsis	Ajuga	Bergenia	Umbrella plant	Lavender
7	Windflower	Rhododendron	Climbing hydrangea	Siberian iris	Saxifrage
8, 9	Veronica	Campanula	Goatsbeard	Monkey flower	Daylily

Note: A discussion of zones will be found on page 4. Some of the plants listed in the milder zones will also survive in colder zones; check with your local garden centre. All plants will grow in zones milder than their first listing; Oriental poppy, for instance, can be grown not only in zone 3, but also zones 4-9.

Notes

5 *Tomatoes*

I don't think anything gives me as much pure gardening pleasure as biting into the first tomato of the season. There's nothing like the smell of a freshly picked tomato, either. If you're used to store-bought, join the growing number of gardeners who find room in their plot for at least one plant. The delicious taste and ease of cultivation will soon convince you that you can't do without a tomato plant or two every year.

You don't even need a garden plot — a tomato plant grown in a container on a balcony can give you enough tomatoes for salads and sandwiches all summer, and maybe enough for some fresh tomato sauce too. And don't overlook those prolific producers, cherry tomatoes. A hanging basket, well watered and fertilized, will keep producing as long as you keep it picked constantly. And how can you resist continually picking the fruit?

I grow my favourite tomato, the Whopper, but I also like to try out new varieties every year just for fun. Roaming through the pages of a seed catalogue in the middle of winter gets my taste buds jumping with their descriptions: "oozing with rich flavour," "a sweet flavour all their own," "sweet dark orange fruits."

Choose tomato plants that are stocky, not leggy or lanky. Look for a good thick stem, as well.

The root mass should just have begun to take on the shape of the pot. You can see the new small white roots.

Facing page: Mouthwatering tomatoes – they're easy to grow. Even a small garden has a corner you can use for a plant or two.

I'm impressed by people who garden in the colder zones of our country and the tricks they've worked out to get luscious tomatoes as early as possible. I'll pass on to you a few of the tips I've picked up from them so you can get the biggest, juiciest, tastiest tomatoes ever!

Planting Tomatoes

What are the conditions that will keep tomatoes happy and provide the optimum yield? Well-prepared soil, deeply dug and with lots of compost added, is the first requirement. The compost will make for soil that drains well, another condition tomatoes prefer. They like to have lots of water on a regular basis and as much sunlight as possible; anything less than six hours of sun will give you a very poor crop. A sheltered spot that warms up quickly and holds the heat is ideal. It's best not to plant tomatoes in the same spot two years in a row.

When you buy your tomato plants, choose ones that are dark green and stocky, not lanky. Check the roots by carefully sliding the plant out of the pot. There should still be lots of soil around the roots, and they should be just beginning to take on the shape of the pot. If you want early yields, choose a variety described as early.

Before we go any further, let's look at the difference between determinate and indeterminate types of tomatoes. Determinate varieties grow to a predetermined height and no more; they produce their crop over a short time and then stop. They usually produce fruit earlier than indeterminate types. Their growth is bushy and they don't require much staking, but you should put down some mulch to keep the fruit off the ground. Indeterminate varieties keep growing until they're killed by frost. They usually need staking and pruning, which involves pinching out growth between the main stem and a branch. This growth is called a sucker and by removing it, you send more energy and nutrients to the fruit. Indeterminates produce fruit for weeks.

To prepare for planting, dig a hole 30 cm (1 foot) wide and deep and fill it with a mixture of equal parts of peat moss and compost or composted cattle manure. In this new mixture, make a smaller hole, just big enough to accommodate the rootball of the tomato plant. You can strip off some of the lower leaves before you put the plant in the hole. Give it a good push so the stem is almost buried up to the bottom leaves. New roots will form along the buried part of the stem, making for a stronger plant.

Add the crushed shells from a couple of eggs (no need to use the insides!) or 30 mL (2 tablespoons) of skim milk powder. This provides calcium — more about that in the section on pests and diseases. Scratch in a handful of 6-12-12 around the plant, being careful not to get any on the stems and leaves. Give the newly planted tomato a good drenching with water — don't skimp! Finally, for

Time for more compost. Tomatoes need lots of moisture, and compost will increase your soil's water-retention.

Amend the soil in the planting hole with a mixture of half and half peat moss and compost.

Dig a hole bigger than the root mass. Strip off the lower leaves; insert the plant into the hole. Scratch in some fertilizer.

Pull up the lower set of leaves so they're not burned by the fertilizer and start to firm the soil around the stem.

• •

those tomatoes that need it, add a stake. As the plant grows, tie the tomato to the stake with pieces of soft cloth or twine so as not to damage the stem.

Care in Spring and Summer

In most parts of Canada, the middle to the end of May is the best time for planting out tomatoes. But some of us like to live a little dangerously and we'll plant out earlier. If you want to take this chance, be prepared to give the tomato plants some special care on frosty nights. In the colder regions, gardeners are almost forced to take these precautions because the growing season is so short. Use cloches or a device called a Wall o' Water to protect

Compost

I love compost. It's so satisfying to run my hands through that crumbly dark mixture that used to be broccoli stalks, eggshells, coffee grounds, potato peels, prunings from plants — even fluff from the dryer. My garden loves it, too.

Most people prefer to compost in a purchased bin or one they've made themselves; in fact, it's not necessary to use a bin, but it does keep the materials tidy. A sunny spot is the best place for a bin; however, a shady spot will do — it will just take longer to work. Add organic material such as chopped fruit and vegetable wastes, lawn clippings, wood ashes, pruned material that contains no disease, and so forth. Do not use fish or meat, dairy products, cat litter or pet excrement, coal ashes, or fatty or oily foods.

You need to layer the materials and to have variety; if you've got a lot of vegetable matter such as leaves or grass clippings, add a layer of soil from the garden. Introduce oxygen into the pile by turning it every week or so. As the micro-organisms start their work, the pile will produce heat. Add a bit of water now and then, especially if the bin is covered. The materials should be like a moist sponge.

In about three months, you'll have the perfect soil amendment that will add trace nutrients, improve the water-retaining abilities of sandy soil, and open up the close structure of clay.

Push the plant firmly into the soil. The buried stem will send out new roots to increase its ability to take in food.

Add two eggshells per plant. The eggshells provide calcium, which helps prevent blossom-end rot.

Start with a 7.5 cm (3 inch) pot so you have a better root mass when you transplant.

tender young tomato plants. Cloches are mini greenhouses that you place over an individual plant to conserve warmth. You can buy commercial cloches — they are usually made of translucent waxed paper, plastic, or fibreglass — but you can make your own. Cut the bottom off a large plastic jug and put the jug over the plant. A stake driven through the handle will secure it and taking the top off provides more ventilation. Heat builds up quickly in cloches, so check the plants frequently on sunny days to prevent them from burning or wilting. Wall o' Water is a device that has plastic pouches joined in a circle. Place the device around the plant and fill the pouches with water. The water heats up during the day and releases the heat to the plant on cool nights. As the plants outgrow these little greenhouses, use light sheets or purchased fabric row covers to cover the plants on frosty nights.

Tomatoes are heavy feeders so fertilize your plants regularly. Use a 10-52-10 fertilizer when planting, then a small amount of 20-20-20 every week. Once a week, water the plants well, soaking them as you did when you first planted. It's important to keep them well watered when the flowers and fruit are being produced and when the weather is hot and dry.

Keep pruning the indeterminate varieties as described earlier. Tomatoes grow quickly, and that includes the suckers, so check them daily and prune accordingly. Pruning also encourages better air movement among the plants, leading to better health. You may also find that the tomatoes will ripen earlier when you prune the suckers.

Pests and Diseases

If you've grown tomatoes before, you might have seen some that had a dark patch something like a scab on the blossom end of the fruit. This condition is called blossom end rot and is caused by a lack of calcium (remember those eggshells?). Another cause of blossom end rot is inconsistent watering or not watering deeply enough. You can eat the tomatoes after cutting off the affected part.

Tomato horn worms, a rather fearsome looking green caterpillar, can be hand-picked or treated with *Bacillus thuringiensis* (B.t.), a bacteria that attacks the insect at caterpillar stage; it is sold in spray form.

If you have trouble with cutworms — they chew through the stems of seedlings, causing the young plants to keel over — put a paper collar around the stem.

When Summer Ends

As the season draws to a close, many gardeners, especially those in areas with short growing seasons, still have green tomatoes on the vine as frost threatens. To help them ripen, remove all flowers and small tomatoes so more energy is directed to the remaining tomatoes. You can also remove the top leaves on indeterminate varieties; this also provides more energy to the remaining fruit.

Another trick is to give the plant a shot of a solution of Epsom salts. Dissolve 30 mL (2 tablespoons) of Epsom salts in 4.5 L (1 gallon) of water. Give each plant 500 mL. The magnesium in the salts helps the fruit ripen.

You can also pick the tomatoes that have started to ripen and set them on windowsills; they will continue to ripen slowly. Other people recommend pulling up the entire plant, including the roots, and hanging it upside down in a warm shed, garage, or basement. And, of course, consider making your own dried tomatoes as well as the usual sauces, salsas, relishes, and juices.

When your harvest is finished, put the spent tomato vines in the compost. Chop them up to help them break down more quickly.

Notes

6 *Water Gardens*

ater gives a feeling of serenity to any garden. Even a simple bird-bath, reflecting the clear blue sky, instantly draws the eye and calms the spirit. There's something mesmerizing about watching the play of light on the surface of water, catching the glint of a golden fish, marvelling at a beautiful waterlily, and listening to the soothing sound of a fountain.

The first step in planning for a water garden is to decide on its purpose. Perhaps you want only a reflecting pond. Maybe you want fish and water plants. What about a fountain or small waterfall? Then look at shapes. Many people like a water garden to look natural and design it with curving edges; others opt for a more formal rectangle.

Choose the site carefully. If you want waterlilies, you'll need a site that gets at least six hours of sun a day. Of course, sun means algae, but I'll give you some hints on dealing with that later. If you want a pond for its reflecting qualities, you can choose a spot at the outer edge of a tree; the image of the leaves reflected in the water will be lovely, but you'll also have to clean the pond more frequently.

A properly installed and well-situated water garden requires little upkeep. After an hour spent deadheading and weeding in the rest of your garden, relax by the pond. You'll never regret putting in this wonderful garden feature.

You don't need a lot of room for a successful water garden.

Plants, fish, water, and pebbles: four complementary natural elements.

Facing page: Water creates a tranquil effect, calming and cooling.

Making a Water Garden

Buy a sheet of flexible pond liner made of polyvinyl chloride (PVC). To figure out the length of sheet you need, add the length of the pool to twice its depth and add 60 cm (2 feet); to figure out the width, add the width to twice the depth and add 60 cm (2 feet). Here's an example for a pond that's 1.2 m (4 feet) square and 45 cm (18 inches) deep.

1.2 m + (2 × 45 cm) + 60 cm = 1.2 m + 90 cm + 60 cm = 2.7 m square
4 feet + (2 × 18 inches) + 2 feet = 4 + 36 inches + 2 feet = 9 feet square

Try to build your pond on a sunny day. Let the liner lie in the sun so that it will be flexible when it comes time to put it in the hole.

Mark out the shape of the pond with an old hose or a piece of rope. Move it around until you're happy with the shape. Then start digging, to the shape you've made with the hose or to the shape of the preformed insert. If you want to have hardy waterlilies, a section of the pond should be at least 60 cm (2 feet) deep. The surrounding sections can be shallower, 35 cm (14 inches) for example, to accommodate other plants. Because you have to backfill with sand, dig the hole 7 to 10 cm (3 to 4 inches) deeper than the planned final depth. Once the hole is deep enough, add a layer of soft sand without any grit or aggregate that is at least 7 cm (3 inches) deep. This will protect the liner from any protruding roots or rocks.

Now spread the liner over the hole. Make sure that it covers the space evenly. If your pond has square corners, fold the material to make as neat a corner as possible. Once you're happy with it, use rocks, bricks, or other heavy objects to secure it at the edges. Start filling it with water, smoothing and adjusting as the pond fills.

To make a neat edge, lift up the sod surrounding the pond and roll it back about 30 cm (1 foot). Slide the edge of the liner under the sod, then roll the sod over the liner. Cover the liner edge with brook stones, flagstones, or brick.

Add a small fountain if you wish. It's not necessary to have it on all the time, and in fact, fish and many water plants are happier in water that is quite calm.

Planting and Stocking the Water Garden

Before you add any plants or fish, let the water garden sit for a couple of days to allow chemicals in the water to evaporate. You're likely to have a problem with algae in the beginning, even after you've done some planting, but don't rush to empty the pond and start all over again. It takes a while to reach balance in a new pond. One type of plant that will help maintain a bal-

It's not necessary to have a fountain running all the time. Use it when you want the sound of moving water.

Hardy waterlilies need 60 to 90 cm (2 to 3 feet) of water in order to over-winter successfully.

Lay a heavy plastic liner over a layer of sand about 10 cm (4 inches) deep. It protects the liner from sharp rocks.

The sod has been pulled back so the liner can be run under it. The sod is then rolled back into place.

. . . .

ance is the oxygenators. These are plants that compete with algae for nutrients, taking nitrogen compounds out of the water. Plants with large leaves, such as waterlilies, also help keep the algae problem under control; their large leaves floating on the water cools and shades the water. Algae need light to bloom, so allowing plants to partially cover the surface of the pond will prevent excessive algae growth. A good rule of thumb is that up to a third of the surface should be covered by plant growth.

When you buy plants for the water garden, such as papyrus, umbrella palm or water iris, they will come in plastic pots, or baskets. Leave the plants in their pots, and place these pots on the liner in the water; arrange them to suit you best.

Ornamental Grasses

One of the newest interests in garden design and planting is ornamental grasses. They make extremely attractive additions to the garden, providing accents, back-drops, and a variety of colours.

Grasses come in every height from 15 cm (6 inches) — blue fescue — to as much as 3.5 m (12 feet)— plume grass. They also come in a great range of colours — all grass in not green! Plume grass, for instance, has grey-green blades on red stems. It turns orange red in fall with sil-very-bronze plumes that become silver in the winter.

Ornamental grasses can play many roles. Make an informal hedge with them. Use them to break up large expanses of single colours. Grow them in containers. Plant sedges at the edges of ponds or other waterways.

Many grasses grow well in dry situations and are welcomed by those of us who are trying to cut down on the excessive use of water. Some grasses that do well in dry areas are mosquito grass, quaking grass, and Siberian wheatgrass.

The grasses can add a dramatic touch to the garden in the autumn, when many other ornamental plants are becoming dor-mant. Left in place over the winter, they not only provide visual interest but help trap snow to help insulate the ground.

Brook stones make an attractive edging but also serve a practical purpose: they hide the edge of the sod.

Fish and waterlilies prefer still water, so put the fountain away from them.

Water hyacinth adds oxygen to the water to prevent algae. It bears attractive mauve flowers if it receives sufficient sun.

Wait for another two weeks before introducing fish to the pond. As I said above, you might have what seems like a severe problem with algae at this time, but as the plants begin to grow and cover the surface, the water should become clearer. You will never entirely eradicate algae, so don't worry if your water isn't as clear as the water from the tap.

It's best not to overcrowd the fish in your pond, so figure on having one fish per 30 square centimetres (2 to 3 square feet). Start with goldfish. Although koi are lovely to look at, they grow quite large and like to munch on the plant life in a pond, such as those waterlilies you've just planted. When introducing the fish into the pond, leave the fish in the container you bought them in — usually a clear plastic bag. Put the container in the pool but do not open it. When it has reached the same temperature as the pool, open the bag and let the fish make its way out. If you've bought fish on a hot day, get them in the pond as quickly as possible; the water in the bag will warm up quickly on your way and could cause the fish great distress, perhaps even death. Give the fish some food. At first they will seem shy and stay among the plants but in a few days they will seem quite at home. Fish are quite sensitive to changes in their surroundings, especially water temperature, so do not add great amounts of cold water if the pond needs topping up. It's best to leave some in a bucket, allowing the chemicals to escape and to take on the air temperature.

Snails are likely to be introduced by hitchhiking in on the plant material you have put in the pool. Over the summer, don't be surprised to see frogs, toads, birds, and other small animals visiting your pond.

Caring for the Water Garden

Once your water garden has been established with plant and animal life, it should be self-sustaining for the rest of the summer. Outbreaks of algae might occur if the weather becomes very hot and the volume of water in the pond decreases considerably. As mentioned above, keep some buckets of water on hand, especially in hot windy weather, to top off the pond.

Don't allow leaves or other debris to settle on the bottom of the pond. In the process of decaying, they will use up valuable oxygen that the fish need even when they're hibernating.

Another problem is that midnight marauder, the raccoon. Even cats are unlikely to do more than watch and dream at the side of the pond, but raccoons often get right in there, turning plants over as they go after the fish. (A good addition to a pond, by the way, is a piece of clay tile, which gives the fish a place to hide when they feel threatened.) Many water gardeners are so devoted to their pond that they bring their plants in every night! Some gardeners stretch a piece of dark netting just under the surface of the water; its holes are large enough to allow fish to come to the surface, but it confuses the raccoon, whose paws have trouble with it. Raccoons are intelligent creatures and will learn there's nothing for them here. Another method to thwart raccoons is to have a screen that you can use to cover the pond with every night. This, however, works only if the pond is fairly regularly shaped.

Pests and Diseases

Compared to many other types of gardening, gardening in water is remarkably trouble-free. If you have fish, they occasionally contract diseases. The store where you bought the fish can advise you on treatment. The pond might be overcrowded or the fish are under stress for some reason.

Mosquitoes that think your pond is a great incubator will soon end up as a tasty treat for the fish. Most of the creatures that come to your pond are beneficial creatures and are not pests.

Winter Preparation

As the leaves start to fall, you will have to be vigilant about keeping them out of the water. Trim plants down to the surface of their pots and put the material on the compost. Hardy waterlilies can be left in place, but tropicals need to go inside for the winter. Check with your supplier regarding other plants you purchased to see what kind of winter care they need.

It is not necessary to completely empty the pond every winter. In fact, once you have the balance established, it's advisable to leave it for as long as it continues to work well. If your pool is more than 90 cm (3 feet) deep, your fish should survive the winter in most parts of the country. They will stay in a state of hibernation until warm weather returns and do not need to be fed during the winter. On the other hand, to be entirely safe, bring them indoors for the winter, following the suggestions for introducing them to the pond — that is, allow them to be acclimatized and don't subject them to great changes in temperature.

You can leave the fish in place and be quite sure they will survive if you add a small water heater for the winter. An air pump keeps the water moving,

Two of the many plants available for ponds: umbrella palm on the left and papyrus on the right.

provides oxygen, and lessens the chances of freezing. You can also lower the level of water after the first freezing by about 2.5 cm (1 inch). Melt a hole in the ice and siphon off some water. Let it refreeze, and then lower the level again. Air is trapped between the two layers and helps to insulate.

In a pond made with a flexible liner, freezing damage is less likely than in a cement or preformed fibreglass pool. However, you might want to float a piece of wood or a container in the pond to help absorb the pressure of freezing water. If the wood or container is a dark colour, it will absorb sunlight and thus become slightly warm, causing thin ice around it to melt.

Another method of protecting the pond in the winter is to cover a third to a half of it with wooden planks, which are covered with a sheet of canvas, then layers of straw, fir branches, or even bags of leaves. Top it off with a sheet of polyethylene. The planks should not touch the water.

If you have fish, never strike the ice in an attempt to open it up. It will produce shock waves that will kill them.

Notes

7 *Pruning*

Picking up a pair of gardening shears can cause the most amazing personality changes, it seems to me. A usually mild-mannered gardener charges off leaving behind a trail of discarded branches and limbs (not human ones!). Normally confident and experienced gardeners freeze with indecision and finally wander away to do something else. There's something a bit scary about trimming and pruning, but I can't think of anyone who's ever killed a tree or shrub by pruning it. It's likely that far more damage is done by not pruning.

Pruning can maintain the health of your plants. It provides better air circulation to the plant, which prevents diseases; it prompts the plant to increase its fruit or flower production; and it improves the shape of the plant.

The home gardener can prune small trees, shrubs, vines, and hedges, but pruning large trees is a job for the experts. They have the equipment to cut out dead limbs and remove live limbs that are inhibiting air circulation and weakening the tree generally and the expertise to bring those often large, and heavy, limbs safely to the ground.

Pruning doesn't have to be a chore, nor does it have to be frightening. I'm going to give you a few guidelines that will make the procedure less

Invest in a pruning saw, which cuts on both the push and pull strokes. A cross-cut saw is not suitable.

Use hedge trimmers to keep cedar in shape. This is one gardening job that can be done at any time of year.

Facing page: Any winter damage sustained by these evergreens will need to be pruned out.

mysterious and daunting. In the end, though, there's nothing better than just getting out the shears — and doing it!

Tools for Pruning

You don't need a lot of tools to get started. If you have only one pruning aid, it should be a pair of hand pruners (also called secaturs, snippers, or pruning shears). These versatile implements are indispensable and many gardeners have their favourite pair handy on every trip around their garden to do a little snipping here, a little deadheading there. Buy the best you can afford.

Use lopping pruners — the ones with the long handles — for getting rid of small branches and large stems.

A pruning saw is necessary for cutting large branches and dead wood. Pruning saws cut on both the forward and backward motion. As I point out repeatedly, don't use a saw from your home workshop.

Other tools useful for various cutting and pruning jobs around the garden include hedge or grass shears and a pruning knife.

What to Prune

Both evergreen and deciduous plants need occasional pruning. Hedges need frequent trimming in the summer, when they're putting on new growth. As fall approaches, your hedge-trimming sessions will be less frequent.

Flowering shrubs, vines, fruit trees, and small trees should be assessed every year to see if they need any pruning. Look for crossed branches, branches growing back into the centre of the shrub or tree, scraggly growth, disease — all of these can be corrected with pruning. Finally, check the shape — you may need to compromise between what looks best to you and what is best for the plant. Although a bowl-shaped shrub might be what you want, it's not very good for the plant because all the growth occurs on the ends of the branches; the inside of the shrub becomes bare and woody.

When to Prune

As a general rule, it's best to prune when a plant is not under stress. For example, don't prune when a plant is setting buds, or when it's going into winter. One of the most important things you need to know about flowering shrubs and vines is whether they bloom on old wood or new wood. Plants such as Deutzia and forsythia that bloom on old wood should be pruned after they've bloomed; plants such as PeeGee hydrangea and Rose of Sharon that bloom on new wood should be pruned in late winter or spring, just as growth starts.

Trim cedar once a year. Hedges should slant outward slightly at the bottom so the light can reach the lower branches.

Flowering shrubs can be trimmed every two years to control growth. Take branches from deep in the shrub.

Tidy up the ends, but avoid the "bowl shape" cut that will result in growth only at the ends of the branches.

This is the lush, healthy growth that results from pruning from within the plant and trimming the ends.

Generally, foliage plants can be pruned at any time except in the fall. Pruning causes the plant to put on new growth and this new growth will be too tender to survive the trauma that winter brings. If your plant needs a fairly major pruning, don't do it all at once. Spread the job over three years, pruning away about a third of the growth each year.

How to Prune

Before you start clipping, walk around the plant to be pruned. Look at it from all angles, identifying any limbs that need to be removed and fixing in your mind the natural shape of the shrub or tree. Check for suckers, new shoots that

Tools

What are the basic tools a gardener needs? You can probably get away with a good spade, a rake, and some hand pruners — and most of you will need a lawnmower. But you'll enjoy gardening more if you have a wider selection of gardening aids. Here are some tools to consider adding to the basics.

Cultivators: Used for weeding, working fertilizers into soil, or cultivating small areas, a cultivator has three or four prongs attached to a long or short wooden or plastic handle.

Garden carts: A garden cart is somewhat more versatile than a wheelbarrow, although it can be a bit more difficult to manoeuvre; it has two wheels, whereas a wheelbarrow has one. The garden cart can carry heavier material than a wheelbarrow and some are angled at the front or have a removable panel for easy filling and emptying.

Trowel: New designs on the market concentrate on comfortable handles, especially for gardeners with arthritis. Trowels can be put to any number of uses: digging, transplanting, planting, weeding. Have several sizes on hand, especially if some of your gardening is done in containers, where smaller tools are more useful. Many trowels now are calibrated which is handy for planting bulbs.

Watering can: Here's where you give yourself a treat. There's nothing like a well-balanced watering can with a good rose (the sprinkling part) to make watering a pleasure. Once a can is filled with water it can be quite heavy, so sometimes bigger is not always better.

The tricky part of pruning: identifying what needs cutting. I don't like the way this lower limb looks, so it gets pruned.

To avoid a nasty tear in the bark, score the under part of the limb before making the cut from the top.

Cut from the top down, at an angle so that a stub will not protrude. It is not necessary to dress the wound.

come from the root or base of the plant. If you have a lilac bush, you'll know of its habit of sending up many suckers. As long as the suckers don't infringe on other plantings, you may decide to leave them, but if the plant is grafted to a different root stock, the suckers will likely weaken the plant's growth.

I'm not very keen on the type of trimming that turns shrubs into shapes they were never meant to be. But hedges are different. They are often used as walls in gardens, defining boundaries and separating sections, so I don't mind seeing them looking quite formal and tailored. Hedges should slope slightly outwards from the top to the bottom. This allows light to reach the bottom parts of the hedge, which otherwise will have fairly sparse growth. As you trim, look for dead branches and twigs and take them out, too.

Try to maintain the natural shape of deciduous shrubs (those shrubs that lose their leaves every year). Start by reaching into the middle and, using hand pruners or a small pruing saw, cut out about a third of the growth. You don't have to do this any more frequently than every other year. As you prune, pause now and then and take another walk to observe your work and be sure you're not getting too carried away. Then, with your shears, trim off any ragged external growth, but leave the shrub with a natural appearance.

Where trees are concerned, the most useful tool is the pruning saw, although loppers can be used on thin branches. Look for branches that cross, especially if they are rubbing together; damaged branches; and low or unattractive branches. These are the parts you will be cutting off. If you feel uncertain about what is "attractive" and "unattractive," take a walk around your neighbourhood, a nearby park, or a botanical garden. Look at the shape of trees. See if you can tell where branches have been trimmed. You'll go home feeling more confident about wielding that pruning saw.

The most extreme example of pruning is topiary, those amazing and fanciful shapes you see in gardening magazines and books but rarely see in people's gardens. You have to be dedicated to maintain these shapes, and keeping a hedge under control is about the extent of disciplined pruning most people want.

Notes
. . . .

Notes

Hard to find perennials shipped potted from coast to coast. David Austin Roses, Clematis, Iris and many choice Hemerocallis. We offer these plus Suttons Seeds and many unusual flowerbulbs in our full colour catalogues published twice a year.

Send us your name and address together with **$4.28 for your 2 year subscription** *(4 catalogues).*

Gardenimport inc.

IMPORTED BULBS, SEEDS & PERENNIAL PLANTS
P.O. Box 760, Thornhill, Ontario, Canada L3T 4A5
Tel.: (905) 731 - 1950, Fax.: (905) 881 - 3499

8 *Lawns*

Many people think of the garden as an outdoor room, an extension of the house. To take this comparison further, the lawn, then, becomes a carpet — a living carpet. It provides softness to the feet and comfort to the eye. It provides a canvas for the passing seasons — in spring, it is lush and a vivid green; in winter, a white expanse; in summer, it reflects the movement of the surrounding trees; and in autumn, it offers a foil for the multi-coloured leaves that fall on it.

Lawns also serve as a frame to flower beds. The quiet, tranquil green of the grass stands in sharp contrast to the riot of flower colours, heights and textures and draws even more attention to the flowering plants than they would receive otherwise.

No wonder we love our lawns — and curse them when they seem to fail us. Some gardeners find lawn care too labour intensive and turn them over to replace them with ornamental plantings. I would never argue that the gardens produced are any less beautiful, but somehow, to me, a garden isn't a garden unless it has some lawn.

Looking after a lawn — cutting, watering, raking, fertilizing — is time-consuming, but I wouldn't give up my lawn for anything.

A good broadcast spreader is essential for distributing fertilizer evenly.

Heavily travelled areas of lawn can be repaired using seed specifically formulated for patching in sun or shade or sod.

Facing page: A lush green lawn: take off your shoes and go for a walk.

Planting a Lawn

If you find yourself faced with planting a new lawn, you'll have to make a decision between seeding and sodding; if you're faced with renewing an old lawn, you'll have to decide whether to dig it up and start from scratch or to patch it up as we show you here. Seeding is inexpensive but the results are slow; sod is more expensive, but it produces almost an instant lawn. The best time to sow grass seed is in early spring or between the middle of August and the middle of September. In milder zones (Zone 7 and up), you can sow from late August to late September. Sod can be laid any time as long as its roots have time to become established. If you are using seed and your lawn is in a great deal of shade, use a mix specially prepared for those conditions. Growing grass in heavy shade is a tricky business.

To start a new lawn — or if you're digging up an old one and starting over — prepare the area well. Take off any existing grass. Dig over the soil to at least 15 cm (6 inches). This is your chance to improve the soil. Work in a lot of compost. Peat moss dug in with the compost will improve the moisture-retentive capabilities of your lawn. As you dig and work at the soil, pull out roots that remain. Any weed roots will grow into new plants as they benefit from the good conditions you're going to give the grass seed or sod. Just before you rake the surface of the lawn, add superphosphate to the soil; it will stimulate root growth. Follow the directions on the bag for the suggested rate of application.

To sow the seed, use a spreader on large lawns; follow the directions on the seed container to guide you in the rate of application. Sowing by hand will be satisfactory on small lawns. Broadcast the seed in a sweeping motion. Lightly rake the seed into the soil so that about half the seeds are barely covered. As much as possible, be sure the seeds are in good contact with the soil. Water the lawn well for at least two weeks, giving it a good soaking every time.

To lay the sod, open each piece of sod and press it into place. Stagger the rows so that seams running crosswise do not meet seams of the next row. Move across the planting area, laying a board on each planted section as you go. When all the sod has been laid, firm it in position by using the board and walking on it or, for larger areas, use a roller. Give the lawn a light raking to fluff up crushed stems, then water deeply. Water well in the first season, especially in dry summers.

Cut the new grass when it has reached about 5 cm (2 inches). Make sure the lawnmower blades are well sharpened to avoid pulling out too much of the growth.

If you're repairing the lawn by seeding it, turn the earth. Take out weeds, being sure to get all the roots, as well.

Cover the spot with about 2.5 cm (1 inch) of grass seed starter. Sow the seed, firm it down and water it.

Before laying sod, rake the soil and add about 2.5 cm (1 inch) of grass starter. Rake the bed again.

Lay the sod a piece at a time. It will sit above the level of the surrounding grass a bit, but it will settle.

Care in Spring and Summer

In the spring, start your care for established lawns by raking them lightly to remove winter debris. Repair any bare patches as I've suggested. Fertilize with a slow-release fertilizer such as 21-7-7. The first number represents nitrogen, so you can see that this fertilizer has a lot of nitrogen, which is just what your grass needs at this time of year. A slow-release urea fertilizer can be applied in early and late spring. Another fertilizer application can be made in the middle of the summer, but it should be a low-nitrogen type such as a slow-release 10-6-4. Don't apply it during very dry weather.

Defining Terms II

Acid soil: Has a pH value of less than 7. Plants that like acid soils are rhododendrons and azaleas.

Alkaline soil: Has a pH higher than 7. Plants that like slightly alkaline soils are delphiniums and clematis.

Compost: Decomposing plant and other organic material that breaks down to produce humus; used as a soil conditioner and mulch. See page 38.

Cutting: A piece of stem or root that is used to developed a new plant.

Dormant: A non-productive resting state in which the plant is alive but is not growing.

Friable: Describes soil that is easily worked and crumbly, perfect for planting.

Hardening off: A process of getting seedlings or other plants used to being outdoors. The plant is left outdoors in a protected area for longer periods each day.

Humus: Decomposed organic material.

Mulch: Material used to cover the soil to conserve moisture, moderate soil temperature, and lessen growth of weeds. Some mulches are organic (pine needles, grass clippings) and some are inorganic (plastic).

Peat or sphagnum moss: Partially decomposed organic material harvested from boggy areas; contains very few nutrients. Peat moss improves the texture of soil. Sphagnum moss comes in sheets and is used for lining hanging baskets or in making living wreaths.

pH: Measures the acidity or alkalinity of soil (the letters stand for potential hydrogen).

Zone: Region with a particular climate. Low numbers indicate colder climates. See page 4.

Firm the sod by stamping on it. The roots of the grass must come into good contact with the soil.

The pieces of sod are laid in alternating strips – the crosswise or end edges do not meet.

Finally, apply a specially formulated fertilizer for sod before watering.

When you cut the grass, keep the blades of the mower set high so that the grass is always at least 5 cm (2 inches) high. This helps to keep weeds under control and helps protect the roots so that they don't dry out as quickly as if the grass were shorter. If you want to rake the clippings, add them to the compost or let them dry before using them as mulch. If you cut the grass frequently, the clippings will be fairly short and can be left where they fall. Cut the grass when it seems to need it. Many of us find our busy lives easier to manage if we can work out a schedule — shopping day, kids' piano lesson day, and so forth — but grass doesn't grow according to a schedule! There are times it will grow quickly and times it will grow much more slowly. If you have "mow the lawn" day on your weekly schedule, be aware that there will be times the grass will be quite long when that day arrives.

Watering is another lawn care task that usually can't be done according to a preordained schedule. Weather is the guide here. Lawns need about 2.5 cm (1 inch) of water a week during times of drought or low rainfall. Windy weather also dries out a lawn so in a prolonged spell of hot, dry, windy weather, you may well want to institute a weekly watering schedule.

If any weeds appear, deal with them at once by hand. Under extreme conditions, when somehow they have got the better of you, use a herbicide as a last resort. Always use such chemicals with great care, following to the letter the directions on the package.

If crabgrass is a problem in your area, treat the lawn with a pre-emergent weed killer early in the spring.

Pests and Diseases

Grubs feed on the roots of grass, causing the plant to die. Look for brown patches and pull at the affected plants. If they come away in your hand, you've got grubs in your lawn. Use an insecticide formulated to eradicate grubs. If the grass doesn't come away in your hand but is still brown, the chinch bug is probably doing the damage and insecticide can control it, too.

Some diseases that affect grass are snow mould and powdery mildew. Both are fungi and are usually temporary conditions. Snow mould occurs on parts of the lawn that have northern exposures. It starts as small straw-coloured spots on the grass, which turn into crusty mats. Break up the threads of the mat with the rake as soon as you notice them and your grass is likely to recover. It's possible to control mildew with a fungicide, but it often disappears on its own in dry weather.

Winter Preparation

In September or October, give the lawn a final feeding with an all-purpose fertilizer. Keep cutting the grass until it stops growing. Because rainfall often increases in the autumn, the grass will grow quite lushly, so you'll probably be mowing more frequently than you did all summer!

Keep the lawn raked, especially as leaves start to fall. Leaves left on grass over winter can become a sodden, impenetrable mat, harbouring diseases and insects and damaging the grass beneath.

Notes

9 *Shade*

Some of the loveliest gardens often seem to have been created under the most difficult circumstances. One of the common "problems" gardeners deal with is what they consider to be too much shade. I don't think shade really is a problem, in fact, and there are many plants that would agree with me.

Frequently the problem isn't shade alone. It's a combination of shade and poor soil or shade and not enough moisture. Look at the type of shade you've got. Is it partial shade — that is, is the garden in shade for only part of the day? Is it solid — shade cast all day by a building? Is it dappled — shade cast by tall trees that allow some light through? With careful selection of plant material, you can have a beautiful garden in any of these conditions — although I have to admit that solid shade is a challenge. If you're dealing with solid shade, consider using containers that can be moved back and forth between the shade and sunnier parts of the garden.

Grass can be difficult to grow in deep shade, so be brave and get rid of it! Plan a growing area full of shrubs, flowers, vines, groundcovers, and other plants that simply prefer to grow in shady locations — and I've got plenty of suggestions for you in this chapter.

The Japanese yew, above, is a member of the large group of yews, which grow well in shade.

Yews also like dry sites, so they make good foundation plantings and have a variety of other uses. They prune well.

Facing page: This hydrangea receives a bit of sun, but it prefers shady locations.

Flowering Plants for the Shade Garden

The plants described below will all grow in partial shade unless noted otherwise.

Two reliable and attractive flowering annual plants for the shady garden are begonias and impatiens. Both can be grown in beds or containers, including hanging baskets. Tuberous begonias like a north or east facing position; they also like rich moist soil. In a bed, don't plant them any closer than 20 to 25 cm (8 to 10 inches) apart. Their flowers come in many forms — single, semi-double, double — and in a range of colours that includes pink, orange, yellow, scarlet, white, and apricot. Impatiens are easy to grow, blooming all summer and requiring no deadheading to keep producing. Plant in rich moist soil about 30 cm (1 foot) apart and don't let them dry out. They also come in a wide variety of colours — pink, white, salmon, orange, magenta — to suit nearly any colour scheme. Both begonias and impatiens are sensitive to frost. Other flowering annuals that do well in the shade are lobelia, browallia, and nicotiana (flowering tobacco).

Plant coral bells about 30 cm (1 foot apart) in well-drained moist soil. They have a long flowering period and even when not in flower, their ever-green foliage is very attractive. Their small flowers, borne on a long stem, are pink, white, or green.

Bleeding hearts, another perennial plant, has ferny foliage that dies down after flowering (if you are a forgetful gardener, mark its position in the garden or you could find you've inadvertently dug it up). The red or white heart-shaped flowers are carried along its arching stem. Give the plant a rich, moist, well-drained soil and it will return year after year.

Foxgloves can grow to 1.5 m (5 feet) and more, so choose your site carefully. These biennial plants like moist well-drained soil. Their tubular flowers are sometimes two-toned with spotted interiors and colour descriptions often reflect this: apricot/bronze, greenish-yellow, pink amber-brown. Other colours sound mouthwatering, such as chocolate and raspberry.

It's hard to know whether to put lily of the valley in the flowering plants or groundcover section — in other words, it can take over. Its sweetly scented white flowers bloom in the spring. It likes a rich well-drained soil and will even grow in solid shade. Another spreader is violets; they like much the same conditions as lily of the valley.

Hydrangea is a flowering shrub that will grow in quite heavy shade. Some varieties can grow to a width of 3 to 6 m (10 to 20 feet), so make sure you have room for it. Give it moist soil and a protected situation. Don't cut it back in the winter, but in the spring, cut it back hard to 7.5 to 15 cm (3 to 6 inches). Its creamy white flowers turn pinkish later in the season and brighten up a shady corner very nicely.

Hydrangea, a useful shade plant, blooms in white, pink, or blue.

Hydrangeas' flower heads are also attractive when dried.

Coral bells is a hardy perennial that will grow in part shade. The foliage adds interest to the front of a border.

The delicate flowers of coral bells are borne on long stalks. They provide a nice contrast in the flower bed.

If you have the proper conditions — light shade and acid soil — give rhododendrons and azaleas a try. They need to be protected from wind and sun in the winter, especially during their first year, but they are spectacular when flowering. They have a shallow root system, so choose their position with care; they don't like to compete for the nutrients in the soil. Their leaves remain green all winter, but to conserve moisture, they curl when it becomes quite cold.

Garden Design

Gardening is a very personal thing — there is no right or wrong way to design your garden, other than being sure to take into account your site and your plant's needs. Nevertheless, many of us feel happier if we have a bit of guidance in these matters. Here are a few handy principles and things to take into account as you survey your "canvas." You'll find that experienced gardeners break the rules at times, but if you're starting out, here are some things to consider.

- Choose a focal point to build your garden around: it might be a statue, trellis, bench, or a spectacular single plant such as a weeping cedar.

- Proportion and scale are important concepts in design. Both involve the relationship between various elements. Small flowerbeds dotted in a large expanse of lawn are out of proportion – a single curving bed would be better. One blazing accent, whether it's a plant or statue, can actually be in proportion in a small garden. Scale refers to matching the size of your plants, garden ornaments, and furniture to your surroundings.

- Plan for a variety of heights in the bed or planting. Place tall plants such as hollyhocks and delphiniums at the back of the border, then medium-sized plants such as poppies and coreopsis in the middle, and short plants such as marigolds and impatiens at the front.

- Colours such as white and grey can be used to blend conflicting colours. Study books, magazines, other people's gardens to see how colour "rules" can be broken.

- Plants are more attractive if they're planted in "drifts" rather than geometrical shapes. Imagine the outline of a teardrop filled with tulips that blends in with another teardrop shape of crocuses. These are drifts. Plants, especially bulbs, look best if planted in odd numbers: five rather than six, for example.

- Live with a new garden for a year before you start designing it. Become familiar with its condition, noting the position of the sun at different times of the year.

- Assess how you will use your garden – and be honest! You might dream of an English cottage garden, but if your kids are at the fort-building stage, you might find yourself at odds with them. Do you need a patio? Where will the garden equipment be kept? What about the compost bin? Do you need a spot for the dog to run? Make a list of the uses your garden will be put to.

- Will you have paths and where will they lead? A curved path is more enticing than a straight one.

- Make yourself a plan! I can't impress on you too strongly the importance of this if you have a dream of what your garden should be. The smaller your space, the more important a design is. It's harder to hide mistakes in small spaces. Use the grid sheets provided in the Appendix of this book to plot out your garden. Draw in your plants in the sizes they will be when they are full grown. As your design takes shape, view the imaginary garden from all windows that overlook the real garden. Refine it until you feel happy, then make it happen!

Foliage Plants for the Shade Garden

Several types of evergreen can be grown in the shade; hemlock is one and yew is another. Yew is versatile, will grow in constant shade, and survives well in urban conditions. Yews like moist well-drained conditions and make good plantings around the foundation of a house.

Two nice shrubs for the shade are highbush cranberry and silverleaf dogwood, the latter doing well in solid shade. The highbush cranberry has white flowers, which are followed by bright red fruit. It can grow to 3.6 m (12 feet) and tolerates wet or boggy soil. Aphids can be a problem with this particular plant. The silverleaf dogwood likes rich soil and plenty of moisture when it's hot or dry, but is quite resistant to pests and diseases. Its pale green leaves have white borders.

Although hostas could be considered a flowering plant, the flowers of this perennial are rather insignificant compared to their foliage. Hostas love the shade and are very effective when planted in masses. The great variety available means that they never have to be boring — foliage can be pale to deep shiny green or gold, have puckered creamy edges, or be what's called glaucous, that is, covered with a bluish-green bloom as plums and grapes are. Slugs are the main enemy of hostas but these plants grow quite lushly and it's easy to cut off damaged growth if you've been unsuccessful in controlling the slugs.

Another group of perennial plants that offers wonderful variety is ferns. You can find a fern for just about any shady situation: moist, dry, or north-facing. If you're looking for interest in the winter garden, search out some of the evergreen ferns. Ferns are quite resistant to pests.

Coleus, an annual plant, grows well in full shade; in fact, too much sun can scorch the leaves. Like hostas, coleus comes in a surprising range of colours — scarlet, pink, deep red, apricot, gold — and leaf shapes. Plant them in the border or use them as container plants. Clip off the flowering spikes to keep the plant tidy. In the fall, take some cuttings and grow them as houseplants over the winter.

Ground Covers and Vines for the Shade Garden

Three perennial deciduous vines that do well in heavy shade are Virginia creeper, climbing hydrangea, and Dutchman's pipe. After being green all summer, Virginia creeper turns a glorious scarlet red in the fall. It climbs by attaching its pads to a rough surface. Climbing hydrangea has large shiny leaves and big white flower clusters with a sweet scent. It clings to surfaces by means of small roots. Dutchman's pipe is a twiner, so lattice or a trellis should be provided for its support. It grows quickly and is often used as a screen. Unfortunately, its pipe-shaped yellowish-brown flowers have a rather nasty smell. All these plants are easily grown and require no special care.

English ivy, a perennial, can be used as a ground cover or as a vine in deep shade. Its glossy leaves stay green all winter. It likes a rich soil that's moist and well-drained. Prune it in the spring, if you want, to get some nice fresh growth.

Japanese spurge and periwinkle are two perennial groundcovers that also like deep shade and have shiny evergreen foliage. Japanese spurge grows upright to about 20 cm (8 inches). It prefers a moist soil and can be planted fairly closely together to give a quick cover. Periwinkle also likes a moist soil. It hugs the ground and, in the spring, sends up pretty little white, blue, or purple flowers.

The Right Plant for the Right Spot

Zone	Part Shade, Moist	Full Shade, Moist	Part shade, Dry	Full Shade, Dry
2	Coral bells	Silverleaf dogwood	Saskatoon serviceberry	Virginia creeper*
3	Bleeding heart	Hydrangea	Pachysandra*	Hemlock*
4	Foxglove	Hosta	Dutchman's pipe*	Yew
5	Rhododendron	Climbing hydrangea	Euonymus*	Japanese kerria*
6	Oregon grape	English ivy	Alpine currant	Box*
7	Clematis	Lily of the valley	Elder*	Golden mock orange*
8, 9	Lady's mantle	Christmas rose	Daylily*	Rock cotoneaster

*Will tolerate these conditions, but will do better with more sun or more moisture.

Note: Some of the plants listed in the milder zones will also survive in colder zones; check with your local garden centre. All plants will grow in zones milder than their first listing.

Notes

10 *Spring Bulbs*

ext to planting seeds, planting bulbs might be considered one of the greatest acts of faith. Most things we plant already have some growth that is above the ground. We can check it every day, assess its health, and wait with anticipation as buds form. But with bulbs, we take something that looks like a shrivelled nut and bury it. We give it some water, try to keep the squirrels away, and believe that in the spring, months from the time of planting, a flower will grow! Fortunately, almost without exception, our faith is rewarded.

When you're preparing your spring garden this fall, start with some faithful old friends such as tulips, daffodils, and hyacinths, then try some of the lesser known bulbs, such as snake's head. Most spring-flowering bulbs seem to open up to the sky, but the snake's head arches over so that the interior of the flower is hidden and we see only the outer sides of the petals, speckled in a pattern similar to a snake's skin.

Whether on the west coast, where small bulbs such as crocus, aconites, and snowdrops can make an appearance as early as January, or on the prairies, where bulbs such as hyacinths barely survive, we look to this group of plants to cheer us up every year, to tell us, in effect, that spring is indeed here.

It's easy to determine the depth of hole for planting bulbs: make it twice the diameter of the bulb.

Plant bulbs pointed end up, giving each a twist as you place it. This will keep them upright.

Facing page: Not all bulbs flower in the spring. Some, such as this beautiful lily, bloom in the summer, and others appear in the fall.

Planting Bulbs

Although some of the plants I'll be describing are not considered to be true bulbs — some of them are tubers, corms, or rhizomes — I'm calling them bulbs. You'll usually find them grouped under bulbs in gardening books, catalogues, and garden centres.

Bulbs are available from garden centres and mail-order suppliers in early fall and it's a good idea to buy them early to get the best choice. Plant small bulbs and daffodils and narcissus when you buy them, any time up until three weeks before the first frost. Wait until October to plant tulips and continue planting until the first frost. If you are unable to plant the bulbs when you receive them, store them in cool dark place that is well ventilated.

Prepare the bed by digging it over well, removing weeds and stones. It's important that the soil be well-drained or the bulbs will rot in the ground. If your soil does not drain well, prepare it a few weeks before planting. The easiest way to solve this problem is to raise the height of the bed by adding good topsoil and compost. Let the bed settle until you're ready to plant.

As you plan your planting, consider the blooming times and periods of the bulbs. You can plant your bulbs in layers if those bulbs are to bloom in sequence. For example, you might plant tulip bulbs that bloom in May in a hole, partially fill in the hole, then plant some snowdrops, which will bloom in March, in the same hole. This is wise use of garden space and especially sensible if you have a small garden.

You can dig a hole for each individual bulb or make a wider hole to take a grouping. The depth of the hole is dictated by the width of the bulb, so the depth of the hole is a little more than twice the thickness of the bulb. Many prepackaged bulbs include this information on the package. However, here are some suggested planting depths for a variety of bulbs:

Crocus: 7.5 cm (3 inches)
Snowdrop: 7.5 to 10 cm (4 to 5 inches)
Glory of the snow: 5 to 7.5 cm (2 to 3 inches)
Hyacinth: 12.5 cm to 15 cm (5 to 6 inches)
Grape hyacinth: 7.5 cm (3 inches)
Narcissus: 15 cm (6 inches)
Scilla: 10 cm (4 inches)
Tulip: 15 to 20 cm (6 to 8 inches)

Sprinkle a handful of bulb food or bone meal in the planting hole. Bulb food is mainly phosphorus, which builds strong roots and prevents disease. Put the bulb in the hole, pointed end up, and give it a little twist to engage it firmly with

Plant the bulbs at least 2.5 cm (1 inch) apart. It's important that they do not touch so that any disease will not spread.

Apply a commercial bulb dust to prevent problems with insects and diseases.

Cover the bulbs with soil and tramp it down. Add more soil if necessary to bring it back to its former level.

Add a layer of mulch to conserve moisture and to act as an insulator during the coming cold months.

- -

the soil. Space the bulbs about 2.5 cm (1 inch) apart. It's important that they do not touch. Sprinkle the bulbs with bulb dust, which you can obtain at garden centres. This will protect them from insects and disease. Cover them over with soil, then firm it in place with your heel. A dusting of rodent repellent will help to protect the bulbs from squirrels. Finally, add a healthy layer of mulch for insulation, then water well — to a depth of 5 to 7.5 cm (2 to 3 inches).

It's a good idea to either label the plantings or keep a small diagram to remind yourself where you've planted those bulbs. It's all too easy in the first flush of horticultural excitement in the spring to start digging without remembering that's the tulip bed you're digging up!

Soil

Soil is more than a medium to hold the roots of plants in place so they don't fall over. Good soil retains nutrients, moisture, and oxygen and releases them to the plant.

What is soil? It's a mixture of particles of rock and minerals; humus, which is dead and decaying material; and air and water. It also provides a home for living creatures such as earthworms and micro-organisms, both of which add to the health of the soil.

Soil is divided into three basic types: sand, silt, and clay. Sand is made up of large particles and will not hold together when you squeeze it in your hand. It is light and loose and warms up quickly but does not hold nutrients or moisture for very long. Clay is made up of very fine particles and will stick together when squeezed. Clay holds water well — sometimes too well! In the spring it warms up slowly but can bake hard in the heat of summer. Its advantage is that it holds nutrients well.

Most garden soil is neither pure clay nor pure sand but lies somewhere between these two extremes. All soils can be improved by adding humus — decomposed organic matter such as dead leaves, kitchen wastes, and prunings from the healthy plants in your garden.

To naturalize bulbs I throw them over my shoulder, then use an iron bar to make a planting hole for each one .

Push the small bulbs into the planting hole, inserting them about 2.5 cm (1 inch).

Using your heel, firm them in place, then replace the piece of sod or scatter some compost over the hole.

Care in Spring and Summer

Bulbs not only make beautiful flowers, but they're low maintenance too. In the spring, all you have to do is appreciate the first signs of green shoots poking through the ground, then wait until the flowers appear. Weeds are unlikely to be a problem, but if any show up, just pull them. If the spring is unusually dry, water the bulb bed. A bit of bulb fertilizer (high phosphate) can be scratched into the ground to feed the bulbs after flowering.

The absolutely vital thing you must not do is cut back the leaves after the flowers have faded. The bulb nourishes itself through these leaves, so they must be left to ripen naturally. When the leaves are yellow and limp, they can be tugged gently away from the plant. Deadheading — snipping off the faded blooms — is fine, in fact, it's advisable, for if the spent blooms are left in place, the bulb will set seed, causing it to exhaust itself. For small bulbs such as snowdrops, scillas, grape hyacinths, and glory in the snow, deadheading is not necessary.

Pests and Diseases

Most bulbs are not prone to disease and pest attack but occasionally you might encounter a problem. Aphids sometimes appear on the stems, leaves, or flowers. Either spray with an insecticidal soap or flush them off with a strong spray of water. Tulips sometimes fall prey to a disease called tulip fire or botrytis. The signs are foliage that has specks that first looked bruised and wet, then turn brown. The petals may become spotted. They can also have this disease after planting, in which case the bulb rots. All parts of the tulip must be destroyed — not put on the compost. Apply a fungicide as a preventative.

Winter Preparation

In the fall, scratch some bulb fertilizer or bone meal into the bulb bed. You may want to put in a new planting of tulips every other year, for tulips are not long-lived — three or four years is the most you can expect. Daffodils, however, will continue to produce for many years if left undisturbed.

Add a layer of mulch, as in the first year.

Naturalizing

I like to see the flowers of small bulbs poking up through the grass in the spring. This practice of allowing them to grow in the lawn is called naturalizing and it's easy to do. Good bulbs for naturalizing are crocuses and scillas.

The Right Plant for the Right Spot

Zone	Sun	Part Sun	Shade	Moist	Dry
2	Glory of the snow	Star of Bethlehem	Lily of the valley	Japanese iris	Grape hyacinth*
3	Blue globe onion	Trillium	Spring snowflake	Yellow iris	Iris reticulata*
4	Grape hyacinth	Crown imperial	Snowdrops	Anemone	Scilla*
5	Crocus	Snake's head	Winter aconite	Jack in the pulpit	Foxtail lily
6	Hyacinth	Narcissus	Trout lily	Spring snowflake	Spring starflower
7	Tulips	Hardy cyclamen	Bloodroot	Calla lily	*Autumn snowflake*
8, 9	*Autumn crocus*	Windflower	Spanish bluebell	Blue water iris	*Ranunculus*

Note: Some of the plants listed in the milder zones will also survive in colder zones; check with your local garden centre. All plants will grow in zones milder than their first listing. Italics denote bulbs that flower in the summer or fall. Some of these bulbs may need lifting in the fall after flowering.

*Will tolerate these conditions, but will do better with moisture.

Notes

• •

....

....

....

....

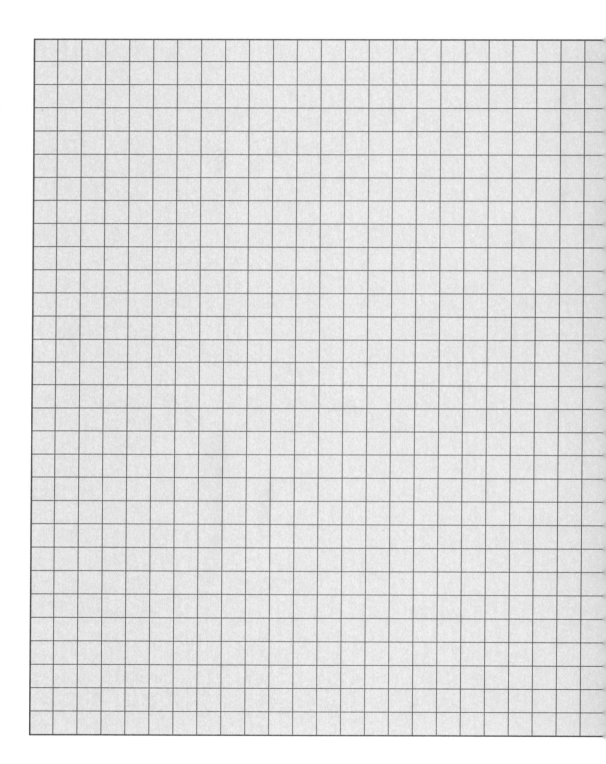

Front Yard Garden Grid

Use this grid to plot out your garden — what grows there now and what you'd like to plant in the future.

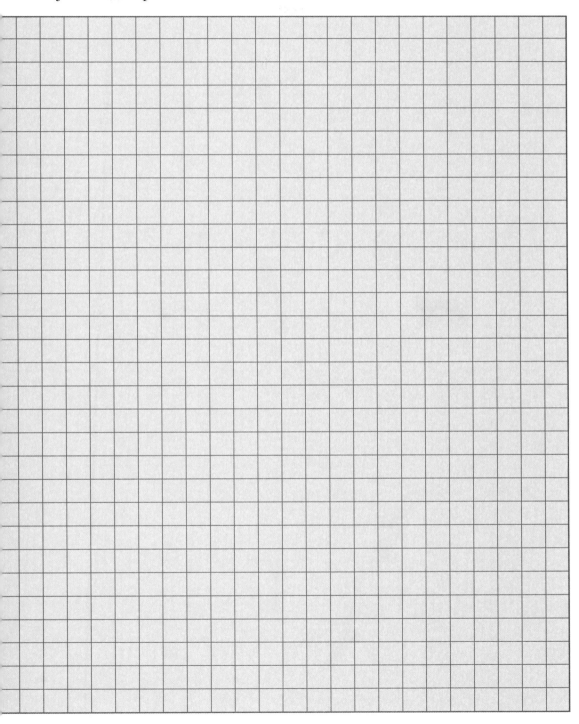

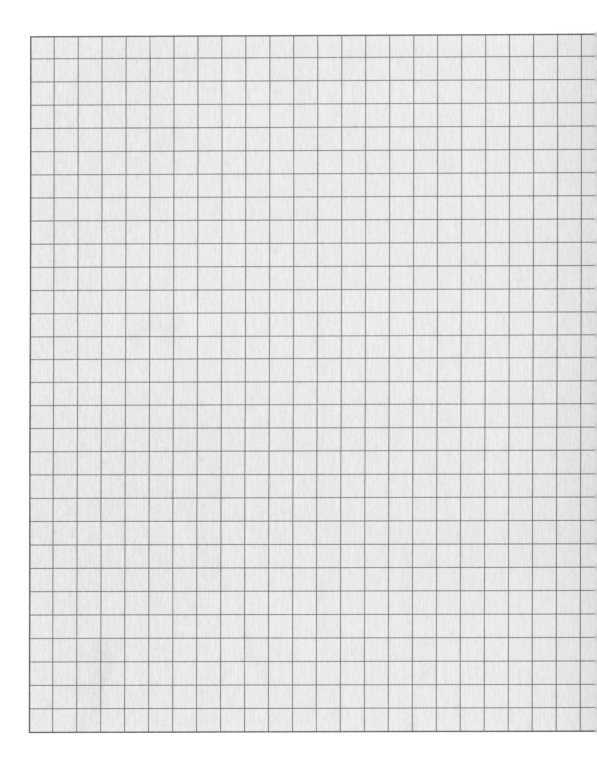

Back Yard Garden Grid

Use this grid to plot out your garden — what grows there now and what you'd like to plant in the future.

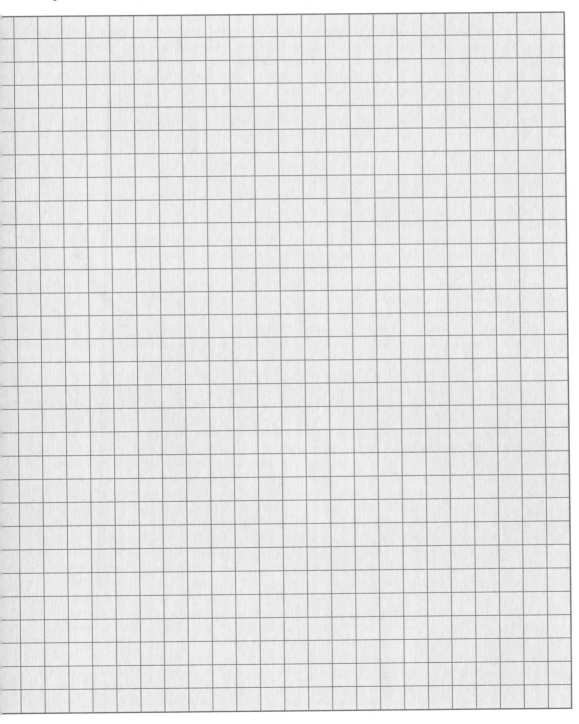

Index

Aconites, 75
Algae, 44-45
Annuals, 68, 71; defining, 20
Aphids, 6, 13, 21, 31, 71, 79
Asparagus fern, 18
Azaleas, 68

Begonias, fibrous, 18; tuberous, 68
Biennials, 68; defining, 20
Black spot, 5
Bleeding hearts, 68
Blossom end rot, 39
Botrytis, 79
Browallia, 68
Bulbs, fertilizing, 79; naturalizing 79;
    planting, 76-77

Chinch bugs, 63
Climbing hydrangea, 71
Cold protection for plants, 37-38
Compost, 2, 3, 5, 10, 22, 28, 36, 40,
    60, 62, 63, 76; making, 38
Coral bells, 68
Crabgrass, 63
Crocus, 75
Cultivators, 54
Cutworms, 39

Daffodils, 75, 76, 79
Deadheading, 5, 21, 29, 79
Designing the garden, 70; ever-
    greens and, 9
Deutzia, pruning, 52
Drying flowers, 30
Dutchman's pipe, 71

Earwigs, 31
English ivy, 72
Enriching soil, 10
Evergreens, planting, 10-11; winter
    preparation, 13-14

Fences, 12
Ferns, 71
Fertilizing, bulbs, 76, 79; ever-
    greens, 13; hanging baskets, 21;
    lawns, 61, 64; roses, 5
Fish, in water gardens, 45-47, 48
Focal point, 68
Forsythia, pruning, 52
Foxgloves, 68

Garden carts, 54
Gardening terms, 20, 62
Gardening tools, 54
Geranium, ivy, 18
Globe amaranth, 30
Glory in the snow, 76, 79
Grape hyacinth, 79
Grasses, ornamental, 46
Grubs, 63

Hanging baskets, 18-22, 68
Hedges, 12; pruning, 55
Hemlock, 71
Highbush cranberry, 71
Hostas, 71
Hyacinths, 75
Hydrangea, 68; climbing, 71

Impatiens, 18, 68

Facing page: Rhododendron likes dappled
shade and acid soil

Contest

Just think how exciting it would be to have a garden expert like Mark Cullen come to your home to help with your garden problems. Bad lawn? Mark will tell you how to fix it! Sad or tired flowers? Mark knows how to make your garden grow! Pruning problems? Let Mark show you what needs to be done! And, that's just what will happen if you are the first prize winner of the Garden Time contest!

1st prize in our Garden Time contest is a visit to your house by Mark Cullen and Dan Matheson with a

THIS COULD BE YOU!

Mark and Dan chatting with a home gardener

Canada am crew! They'll bring with them $1000 in gardening supplies. And, their visit to your house will become one of the Canada am Garden Time show segments in 1996! (Total prize value $1000.)

2nd prize is $500 worth of gardening products-fertilizers, weed killers and tools.

3rd prize is a gift certificate from Gardenimport inc. worth $250. so you can pick from the beatufiul Gardenimport mail order catalogue of bulbs, seeds and perennials.

Send in your entry now!

• •

CONTEST ENTRY FORM

Please send this form, a hand-drawn facsimile of this form or a postcard with your name and address to:

Garden Time contest
c/o INFACT Publishing Ltd.
66 Portland St., 2nd Floor,
Toronto, ON M5V 2M8

Name: _____

Address: _____

Town/City: _____ Province: _____ Postal Code:_____

Telephone: Day: _____ Evening: _____

Draw to be held 2 p.m. Jan. 31, 1996. Contest details on reverse.

How To Enter

Clip the entry form out, fill it in and send it to: INFACT Publishing, 66 Portland St., 2nd Floor, Toronto, ON M5V 2M8. The draw, from all forms received, will be held Wednesday January 31, 1996 at 2:00 p.m.

Rules

1. Residents of Canada 18 years of age and over may enter, except employees and immediate family members (and/or persons domiciled with) of CTV Television Network Ltd., INFACT Publishing Ltd., Weall & Cullen Nurseries, Canadian Tire Corporation and prize suppliers.
2. Entrants may enter more than once provided that their entries are on the Contest Entry Form or a hand-drawn facsimile. No photocopies.
3. The chances of one entry being drawn depends on the total number of entries received.
4. Winning entrants will be contacted by phone and must correctly answer a time-limited skill testing question.
5. Winners must agree to their names and photos being used for publicity purposes and to sign a waiver on behalf of CTV and INFACT Publishing.
6. Prizes must be accepted as described with no cash substitutes.
7. The decision of the contest judges is final.

• •

Watch for . . .

Garden Time Volume 2:
More to Know About Gardening

another exciting book and video set by

Mark Cullen
with Dan Matheson

Including:

- growing plants from seed
- preserving annuals for replanting next summer
- gardening projects for kids
- how to pick a Christmas tree
- winter flowers to grow
- caring for house plants
- and much more!

Coming
Fall 1995